Ezra and Hadassah: A Portrait of American Royalty

HEATHER YOUNG

Ezra and Hadassah: A Portrait of American Royalty

First Printing 2013

Copyright@2013 Heather Young

To protect their privacy, names of several individuals have been changed. Most are innocent victims, but a few are guilty as sin. Since I have no intention of being sued, it will be obvious as you read who is a good guy and who isn't.

For more information:

Ezraandhadassah.blogspot.com

For Rob, who was right.
This is harder than we thought.
Thanks for doing it anyway.

CONTENTS

1. THE GOOD OLD DAYS

My first memory of life doesn't begin with my biological parents. My memory begins at the foster home, an old-fashioned four-story craftsman style house with a wide front porch located near downtown Portland, Oregon. I rode a tricycle on the sidewalk in front of the house, my two year-old brown hair ruffled by the wind. At that point I spent my days at the foster home while my brother went to Head Start Preschool. Ezra and I went home to our parents every night, like any other children in daycare. We weren't yet living full time at the foster home - that would come within another year or two. I had no idea we were far from typical.

That knowledge would unfold slowly, year by year as my body and brain grew and my awareness of a world beyond my tricycle on the sidewalk expanded. In the beginning, I knew only the sensation of the worn rubber on the front wheel of the tricycle bumping unevenly on the pavement as I raced an imaginary foe to the end of the block, stopping just short of the curb dumping me into the street.

By the time I was five years-old, I knew. I can't explain how or when I knew, maybe at some point an adult sat me down and gently explained my life in a way that I was able to understand. If they did, it was such a non-conversation I can't recall it. There is an equally good chance no adult said anything and I just put the pieces together myself. I knew our mother Claudia had something called schizophrenia and our father, Ralph was referred to as developmentally challenged. I knew they couldn't take care of us. There was no drama, no police, no ripping me from my parent's arms. Just one evening our parents didn't come to get Ezra and me and we didn't go home that night. Silently we flipped from visiting the foster home to visiting our parent's home.

The neighborhood around the foster home felt safe to me. I considered the streets surrounding it to be my home as much as the actual house. It was a working class community, all the houses lined up in rows with narrow paths between each. The sidewalks in front were perfect for bike riding and roller-skating. Across the street from the foster home a group of houses were bought by several families. I watched them turn their homes into a communal living, hippy kind of thing. Kids roamed freely in and out of all the houses, being fed and disciplined by whichever adult was nearby. The fences separating backyards were torn down and the area in the middle of the block became a shared garden and playground. I loved hanging out with the hippy families because they were nice to me and invited me to their children's birthday parties. It was fun, even if all they ate were salads.

Our foster home had a partially finished attic that became my indoor refuge, a place to escape to when I needed a break from living with foster parents and seven or more rotating children. The attic ceiling was tall enough in the center for an adult to stand comfortably and it had plenty of natural light from the big windows on all four sides. The middle of the floor had plywood across the exposed beams covering the crumbling insulation between the floor joists. A metal railroad train set with tons of track and miniature village pieces occupied hours of my time.

I lay on the floor, my face pressed into the dusty film, so I could get the best view of the tiny people as they moved around their orderly town. The miniature townspeople got on and off the trains that took them over mountains made from cardboard boxes and tunnels constructed from old oatmeal tubes. It wasn't the trains that fascinated me. Actually, the way their tiny wheels constantly fell off the track annoyed me. It was how the sun, streaming in from the windows, fell across the town illuminating the ancient dust specks in the air. The flakes of dust gently settled on the post office, the school, and stores like freshly fallen snow. It was a peaceful village of people with happiness painted on their faces. I could imagine myself living there someday, running the beauty shop or the deli. It was a calming scene, full of everyday life with no surprises. Everyone did what was expected without shouting, hitting or drama.

The second floor of the foster home consisted of a bathroom and three bedrooms. Our foster parents, Dorothy and Wayne shared the master bedroom, the girls shared one bedroom and the boys the other. Since we had no closets or dressers in our bedrooms, the kids' rooms had plenty of space for several rows of bunk beds in each. There were two extra beds for 'short-timers'. They were kids who came for a few days or months at a time, knowing they were not here to stay. I always felt sorry for those kids, they were lower on the list than I was. At least I had a place to be.

The thing about short timers is they never had luggage. Their clothes and shoes and toys were always transported in brown paper grocery sacks. I thought that was terrible. I knew I would have a suitcase of my own when Ezra and I grew up. We planned to move into the tree house I was going to build. We were going to live by ourselves in the forest and never be dependent on anyone ever again.

Leading to the basement laundry room, where everyone in the house had their clean clothes folded and stacked on shelves, was a door covered in names. The names were scrawled in pen, pencil, crayon and marker. It was like a genealogical diagram of names from all the foster children who had lived there over the years. To me it was a daily reminder that I was one of many, most of whom I had never met and never would. When I learned to print my name, I added mine to the door in red block lettering – HADDIE. It wasn't a point of pride for me. It wasn't like adding a line to a family growth chart or anything like that. It was more a stubborn declaration of my existence. All I really wanted in life was to be noticed, to be counted. Adding my name to the door meant I was real. I was somebody.

Living as a foster child means the quality of your existence relies on the moods of those you share space with. If it goes particularly bad for even one day, you can be packing your bags the next day, forced to leave over something you had no control over. On the good days, the carrot of possibly making you a permanent member of the family is dangled, only to be yanked away on the next down day. It is not unlike a yo-yo, constantly going up or down, never staying still.

Our foster father Wayne had a problem. I didn't know what it was but I knew enough to stay away from him in the evening as he lined up empty beer bottles. I watched heated arguments between Dorothy and Wayne about him needing to get a hold of himself. After a while Wayne would dismiss Dorothy with a wave and stagger upstairs to bed in response to her nagging. Wayne mostly sat in the dining room, hunched over his CB radio equipment, talking to truckers on the road and drinking beer. Occasionally he would let me use his CB mike to talk using the handle 'Dandelion,' a name I gave myself because I loved the only flower no adult would yell at me for picking.

Wayne didn't have patience with anyone but he particularly found my brother Ezra annoying. Ezra was unable to figure things out for himself; he cried and threw temper tantrums when he was ignored. Wayne couldn't tolerate Ezra's helplessness and spanked him often for not shutting up his bawling. Ezra got spanked hard enough, often enough, that he wet his pants in anticipation of a spanking.

Ezra's hard times were not confined to the foster home. School was another minefield of intimidation and threats of violence. One morning before the first bell rang, I found Ezra surrounded by a group of menacing older kids. His fists were up in a defensive stance and he was obviously scared. I pushed through the bodies and put myself between the crowd and my brother. I yelled, telling them to leave him alone. I was karate kicking at the crowd when we were rescued by a recess aide who took me to my kindergarten teacher, telling her I needed a treat for bravery.

My kindergarten teacher used corporal punishment in class. If a child misbehaved, she took them to the front of the class and put them over her knees to spank them. One day I was in wide-eyed, frozen shock while I watched her pull a boy over her knees and at the last second, pull down his pants and spank him bare-bottomed. I was embarrassed for him and terrified of her. I was on my best behavior for the rest of the school year, afraid I would be next. The last few weeks of class that teacher disappeared, replaced by a substitute. The rumor was the parents of the boy who was paddled bare-bottomed had complained.

The question I dreaded at the beginning of every school year was "Is Ezra your brother?" I knew I would be judged based on their opinion of him. More than once I overheard teachers talking about me, saying, "She's nothing like Ezra. You won't have any problems with her." I was an average student, but I excelled with teachers. I learned my first year of school how important it was to get on the teacher's good side and then work like crazy to stay there. I was looking for an adult who would like me.

I was in my first grade class laboring over a worksheet copying the letter F when a grown-up came into the room and talked to my teacher. They both turned to look at me. "Haddie? Could you come here please?" my teacher asked, motioning me out into the hall. Stooping to my eye level, my teacher said, "Your brother is having a hard time this morning. Do you think you could go talk to him?" I nodded, wanting to please my teacher. I was taken to my brother's classroom by the grown up, where Ezra was crouched under his desk, barking and growling like a dog. The teachers were hoping I could coax him out from under the desk. I tried talking to him, but all the kids in the class were staring at us and I was humiliated and scared by my brother's behavior. All I could do was cry and I was taken back to my class. I was never asked to help with Ezra again.

Being liked by my teacher was a way for me to feel secure at school, knowing someone would watch out for me if any kids gave me a hard time. I was never a target for bullies the way Ezra was. I was constantly on alert for mean kids at recess and lunch, determined to protect my brother.

In first grade I took Wayne's Swiss Army pocketknife to school. I saw it on his CB table, where he left it after using the blade to clean his fingernails. I slipped it into my pocket before school without anyone noticing. The handle was bright red and felt smooth and heavy in the front pocket of my favorite jeans. During a bathroom break I took it out and showed a couple of girls from my class. I didn't open the blade, my fingers weren't strong enough to pry open the edge. I just thought it looked cool and I wanted kids to know I was brave enough to have a pocket knife. It took less than twenty minutes for my teacher to send me to the principal's office. I had never been there before and I was very worried.

The principal motioned to me to stand next to her desk as she leaned forward. "Do you know why you are here?"

I shook my head no.

"I understand you brought a knife to school today. Is that correct?"

I hesitated, then nodded.

She asked very calmly, "May I have it?" and extended her hand. I reached in and withdrew the knife, feeling its exquisite heft again. I liked the smoothness of the knife case, as soft as a rock washed by river water rushing over it for eons of time. She took it and invited me to sit in a chair outside her office. A few minutes later Dorothy showed up at school and spoke to the receptionist. I knew I was in trouble. I put my head down and stared at the floor.

"Why did those girls tell on me? I didn't do anything. I

wasn't going to hurt anyone." I thought, angrily. The knife was just cool, a Show and Tell item. The fact it made me look tough was just a plus. No one was going to mess with me the way they did with Ezra.

Soon enough Dorothy and I were in the principal's office together, with the principal giving Dorothy the details. Apparently, taking a pocketknife to school was a big deal. Dorothy looked horrified and asked, "Where did you get this?"

I explained where I got it from and that I wasn't doing anything bad. The principal asked if I had ever brought the knife to school before and I said no. Then she asked if I had ever carved into the bathroom walls at school using the knife. I hotly said no, insulted at the suggestion. I pointed out I couldn't even open the blade. Both the principal and Dorothy tried to open it for themselves and agreed it was unusually difficult to open. My logic won out and after a lecture about bringing knives to school, I was allowed to go back to class. If I could have guessed the trouble I would get into with his pocket knife, I would've swiped the other cool thing on Wayne's table, his pipe. I just figured he would miss his pipe before he noticed his pocket knife was gone.

By lunch time a rumor circulated that I tried to stab someone in a bathroom brawl. I denied fighting, but also didn't fully explain the situation. It worked to my advantage to be perceived as slightly menacing. The downside was I didn't get invited over for play dates at the 'nice families' houses. By first grade I was already considered a little too wild for the genteel mothers' liking.

I was six years-old when I decided to run away. I couldn't live with the new rule stating that we had to have a buddy when going outside the foster home to play. It was too much. My wings were clipped; I could no longer roam the deserted streets early in the morning or stay outside for hours all by myself. Now I had to have a buddy with me at all times. That wasn't going to work for me. I told my brother we were running away and he said ok, as long as we could go after he finished watching The Mickey Mouse Club Show. I agreed and while I was rummaging in the kitchen for our running away food, I caught Barney, another foster kid, heading out the back door without a buddy. I told him Ezra and I were leaving.

"Oh yeah?" Barney said. "Where are you going?"

"We're getting out of here. We're running away." I showed Barney my bag full of food and suddenly I had his full attention.

He was a year older than me and much taller. Barney was my loyal sidekick in my daredevil play. We delighted in climbing the highest trees and dangling on the thinnest limbs, far surpassing any other child on our block with our agility and fearlessness. We foster kids affectionately called him Barney Google with the goo-goo-googely eyes because he wore thick glasses and both of his eyes were lazy and tended to drift in their sockets. Barney was also well respected by the neighborhood kids because he ate live ants off the sidewalk and declared them delicious. Barney didn't ask me why we were leaving and neither did my brother.

All I wanted was to tell Dorothy about the man standing in the doorway of the men's restroom, which faced the playground. He had longish brown hair and very deep red brown skin like a person who was outdoors a lot. His pants were down around his boots, his hands moved jerkily over his privates. I was swinging, pumping my legs and arching my back as far as possible, trying to touch the sun high in the sky with my outstretched pointed toe. When I saw the man standing in the doorway, I abruptly stopped swinging by digging my toes into the soft sand underneath the swing and in the ensuing cloud of dust, I ran away. I wasn't sure exactly what the man was doing, but I knew enough to know I didn't want any part of it.

I had already created a barrier between myself and one of my foster father's creepy friends. That guy would come around to the foster house to drink beer with Wayne. He was a grown man with a wife and little children of his own. The way he looked at me made my skin crawl.

One day all of us were at his house for a cookout and I had to use the bathroom. He volunteered to take me. He walked me past the washroom in the hallway, back to the bathroom off his master bedroom. He motioned me in. I shut and locked the door behind me. Next to the toilet was a stack of Playboy magazines. As I sat on the stool and looked at the pile of dirty magazines, I was mad at his wife for letting him have those in the house with their children. She shouldn't allow her husband to have that in their house. The pictures on the magazine covers were gross. As I exited the bathroom the man was standing in the bedroom waiting for me.

He wanted to show me something special in his closet. I told him "No" and ran out as fast as I could, him calling after me. When I got back into the crowd in the backyard I made sure I was buried in the pile of laughing and screaming children. I could hear him complaining to adults that I was a big brat and a tease.

Wayne called me over to apologize to his friend because I hurt the man's feelings. I looked up into his pouty face and mumbled a lame, "I'm sorry." and ran off to play before the adults could ask anything else of me. I just wanted get as far away from that man as possible.

The man doing nasty things to himself in the park made me feel like Wayne's friend. I wasn't about to tell Dorothy or Wayne what I thought about his friend because I wasn't going to get punished for being sassy, but I knew the man at the park was safe to tell on. That was all I wanted Dorothy to know. I didn't mean to get myself locked into dragging someone else around with me. This new buddy system would hold me back and ruin my routine.

Every morning at the foster home, I was up and out with the early sunrise. I liked being at the park before anyone else. My favorite part of the tree-filled park was a cement-lined circular wading pool that started at the edges just barely covering my toes and then deepening to knee high in the middle. I could get out of the summer heat and didn't even need a swimsuit. The only authorities at the wading pool were the parents of the little kids and babies. I was careful not to splash them, so no one gave me a hard time. It was a beautiful, free place to relax and forget my life.

At six years old, I already had a lot to forget. The foster home was chaotic, with no rules and no schedule. I floated from day to day, avoiding contact with the adults, especially Steve and Mark, Dorothy and Wayne's biological teenage sons. Steve had his pad decked out in the basement where a regular stream of pot-smoking kids hung out.

Steve invited Mary, another foster kid, down to his room. I was jealous of her because he never allowed any of us kids into his private den, which had a couch, a stereo and strings of lights hung from the rafters. I don't know exactly how it happened but I found out Steve was messing around with Mary, who was a year older than me and mentally slow.

It wasn't long after discovering his Naked Games with Mary that I was invited down to Steve's room and inducted into his "secret club" by swearing I would never tell anyone about it.

I just wanted Steve to like me. He didn't care about the foster kids and treated us like bratty nuisances. I wanted a big brother who would play with me and take me places in his car.

After I agreed to not tell, Steve played Naked Games with me. Soon enough Mark found out what his brother was doing to us girls and he joined the secret club too. Now I had two brothers wanting to spend time with me but not in a way I wanted. I was stuck. I didn't like their secret club. I was repulsed by their bodies and the things they wanted me to do, but I wasn't slow like Mary.

She thought they really liked her. She would pout and throw little fits if Steve or Mark didn't take her for car rides or ask her to watch tv with them in Dorothy and Wayne's bedroom when the adults were out of the house. I didn't understand a lot of things, but I knew I had no choice. I was ashamed, not of the Naked Games, but by being so stupid to get myself trapped.

Even at six, a child barely able to print the alphabet, I

knew the rules. I was the foster kid, the disposable one. As a foster child you have no power. You are living at the whim of others. If you rock the boat, accusing the real children of bad things, they wouldn't be the ones leaving, you would. I couldn't risk losing what little security Ezra and I had. I didn't want Dorothy and Wayne, or Ralph and Claudia to blame me for messing things up. I didn't want to live in a different foster home. Even though I certainly didn't like where we were, I was used to it. The devil you know is always better than the devil you don't know.

Nineteen seventy-four was a good year to run away. No one stopped us, three children ranging in age from six to eight years old, each with a school backpack filled with our treasured childhood things. We had a great day wandering neighborhoods we had only previously seen from the car as we sped by. The sun was shining brightly as the deep green leaves from the trees hanging overhead absorbed the heat, cooling us as we walked. The adults we passed while on our great escape were very pleasant. They offered their garden hoses when we asked politely for a drink. No one questioned three small children walking by themselves. Back then it wasn't illegal to be on an adventure.

Everything was going perfectly until dusk, when Ezra started complaining his feet hurt, he was hungry, he wanted to watch tv and couldn't we just go home? Barney chimed in with his own list of gripes and I slowly realized it was one thing to take off on your own but a whole different thing when you are responsible for others. They had way higher expectations than I did.

I was looking for a porch we could sleep on for the night, determined not to return to the shackles of foster hood. My compatriots on the other hand, would have none of that and when Ezra burst into a full-fledged temper tantrum, I gave in to their demands. We slowly wandered home well after dark.

As we turned up our street I saw multiple police cars with blue and white lights flashing, parked at our end of the street. I panicked, thinking something bad had happened while we were gone. We began jogging, hoping everything was ok.

On the street in front of the house all the neighbors crowded around Dorothy. Her eyes were bloodshot from crying, her voice cracking with hysteria. Someone spotted us coming and a shout went up. That was when I knew I was in big trouble. The crowd parted and I was hustled up to the police cars. Until then my only motivation had been, "They don't think I am big enough to take care of myself. I'll show them." I hadn't considered the consequences of failure. Few six year-olds do.

Dorothy grabbed up Barney and Ezra in a huge hug, saying we scared her to death, blah, blah, blah. We answered a couple of questions from the police and were sent off to bed because it was almost midnight.

I was cautious the next morning. I was worried I would get spanked the way Ezra got spanked, hard enough that he wet his pants. Other than being grounded to the house indefinitely and lectured until Wayne asked for a beer, nothing happened to me. My brother and Barney pinned everything on me, as I expected. I wasn't mad at them. The escape attempt was my idea and I was stubbornly proud of it.

When Dorothy asked why I wanted to run away, I said, "Because you won't let me go to the park alone anymore."

She looked at my sincere face and sighed. "Haddie, are you going to learn everything the hard way?" she asked, not really expecting an answer which was good because I had no idea what she meant. Learn everything the hard way? I was killing myself just trying to survive the jungle I already lived in. After a moment of silence I went into the living room and sat down on the floor next to Ezra who was contentedly watching The Electric Company, a PBS show that starred a funny guy named Morgan Freeman.

I learned a valuable lesson from my first attempt to escape my cage. If I wanted to run away, I needed to plan ahead. Since I couldn't leave my brother behind and he wouldn't accept sleeping on anything other than a bed, preferably with a tv nearby, running away and living on the streets was not an option for us. No matter what, we were stuck for the duration.

2. OUR DISAPPEARANCE

Ezra and I had been living at the foster home full time for three years. Early in the year we began having visits from state workers I hadn't seen in a while. They played with me and Ezra and asked how we felt about the foster home and our real parents. We told them we were fine living with Dorothy and Wayne at the foster home during the week and spending weekends with our biological parents, Ralph and Claudia. We were different than the other foster kids because we got to leave for the weekends and they didn't.

The thing I liked best about our real parent's house was that it was quiet. I could go out in the back yard and lie in the grass, watching bugs scurry about, carrying leaves ten times as big as themselves or dragging the carcass of a dead fly across the driveway and then stuffing the body into a crack in the pavement for safe keeping. Even when I watched a spider catch a bug in its web and slowly wrap it like a burrito in its sticky string, I was at peace. I wasn't listening to hear if my name was called and what tone was being used. I didn't hear yelling, screaming or fighting. I heard only the stories I made up in my own head as I imagined myself as a butterfly or inch worm or potato beetle.

The house itself was a simple plain white bungalow with three bedrooms so Ezra and I had our own rooms. My bedroom overlooked the front of the house and had lovely windows shaded by big trees in the yard. During the summer when it stayed light past my bedtime, I imagined climbing out on the tree limb nearest my window and then shimmying down the tree to the street, free to continue playing as I wished. I never did it, but I spent a lot of happy time strategizing how I could do it.

The pink table lamp next to my bed had plastic angels with wings watching over a small door. When I turned the knob two clicks, a nightlight shone through the translucent plastic door and I could look at picture books in bed before I fell asleep. My room was plain and clean and all mine. I didn't have to share anything. I didn't have to be on guard, careful to not touch anything that belonged to someone else.

Weekends with Ralph and Claudia moved at their own, slower pace. It was nice because living at the foster home felt like dog-eat-dog, survival of the fittest. At Ralph and Claudia's we weren't hit and no one yelled at us. They didn't even use swear words. The worst thing was complaints from the neighbors that we wandered the neighborhood too freely and looked like we didn't take baths often, which was true, because Ezra and I both held the opinion that baths were a waste of time, soap, and water. We took mandatory baths once a week at the foster home, always on Sunday early evenings after our 5 p.m. return from Ralph and Claudia's. It was timed so we didn't miss a minute of The Wonderful World of Disney on NBC at 7 p.m.

Apparently our hatred of bathing was genetic, because Ralph and Claudia both struggled to put on clean clothes and to take showers. They didn't see the need for personal cleanliness, which was my only problem with them. They stunk, really badly. Their hair was greasy and they went days and days without changing clothes. Both of them had bad teeth and terrible breath. I hated having to get near them for hugs and kisses because they smelled so bad. I didn't like bathing either, but I always wore clean enough clothes and I didn't think my kid body stunk like an adult's. Adults should know better. Other than that, spending time at their place was fine. I was happy being at their house, just not necessarily being with them.

The weekend highlight for Claudia was taking us across the street on Sunday mornings to her church, the Jehovah's Witness Kingdom Hall. I hated church. It was two hours of sitting still and being quiet while adults standing in front of the congregation preached away. The only thing that made it bearable was that the walls were adorned with a panoramic landscape painting of the earth with animals and beautiful flowers and trees. I think it was supposed to represent earth when the End Times come and the earth is cleansed from wickedness. I spent a lot of church time staring at the walls, pretending I was in the forest with the peaceful lions lying next to sleeping lambs.

The one time I felt uncomfortable at my parent's house happened when I was five. I was looking for Claudia and called out her name. She opened the bathroom door and motioned me in. She was sitting on the toilet, reading one of her many books. Claudia invited me to sit on her lap so she could read aloud to me while she continued her bodily functions on the pot. That weirded me out and I declined her beckoning wave. She called after me as I ran out the front door, "Haddie, you don't have to be afraid. I'm just going to read to you." I refused to sit on her lap after that, clothed or not clothed.

We didn't call Dorothy or Wayne our parents and we didn't call Ralph and Claudia mom and dad. They were just their first names to us, grown-ups who took care of us.

One day at the foster home a visiting social worker asked us "What would you think of having a family of your very own, one that you can live with all the time?"

I didn't know what to say. I had no concept of what she was talking about. All I knew is what we were living felt weirdly temporary and yet permanent at the same time. I knew Ezra was desperate to get away from Wayne's spankings and I was all for an adventure so we agreed that it sounded fun to have a new family.

I showed off my tree climbing skills to the social worker

as she took pictures of me. I didn't question why Ezra and I were getting regular visitors who wanted to talk to us and asked us to draw pictures of our foster home and Ralph and Claudia's house. I thought they liked our art. The other foster kids were jealous and I loved the adult attention. Finally someone noticed I was nice and special and wanted to spend time with me.

That summer a new social worker showed up and instead of talking to us, he told us to gather our clothes and put them in his car. We didn't have suitcases so our clothes were folded by Dorothy and put into brown paper grocery sacks. Besides our clothes, we were told to choose only three personal things to take, nothing else. The rest of our belongings were to stay with the other foster kids and at our real parent's house.

First I chose my record and storybook combo from the movie "Bedknobs and Broomsticks." When I was four years-old Ralph and Claudia took me to the movie theater to see the Disney movie. I discovered the wonder of padded theater seats and Flicks chocolates, a brightly colored cardboard tube stacked with chocolate pieces that melted slowly, one mouth-sized piece at a time. They bought me the long-playing "Bedknobs and Broomsticks" record and read along storybook to remember the event. Before I packed the record and story book, I wrote in my best printing my name and Ralph and Claudia's names and their address on the back cover, just in case it got lost in transit.

I also brought a white vinyl purse because it was a hand-me-down from Claudia and it had their address written on an inside flap. I thought it would be good to have that information when we were ready to return home to them. They were our parents after all, so of course we would be coming back to them. The last thing I packed was my Mrs. Beasley doll, the one that came with granny glasses, polka-dotted cloth legs and a string on her side that talked when I pulled and released it. I also asked to have a crocheted teddy bear that was at Ralph and Claudia's but the social worker told me there wasn't time to get anything from their house.

The night before we left, Dorothy came to my side at bedtime. She hugged and kissed me, telling me she loved me. I was elated and I didn't want to ever leave because until that night, I had no idea she loved me. She had never hugged or kissed me or touched me beyond taking take care of my physical needs. I had no reason to think Ezra and I might be loved by Dorothy or anyone else in her home. Now that she said she loved us, I wanted to stay. I craved love. To think Dorothy actually loved me! It seemed like a miracle come true. And now we were leaving? It didn't make sense to me at all. And what about Ralph and Claudia? Ezra and I spent nearly every weekend with them while we lived at the foster home. Why couldn't that continue? Why did we have to leave everyone behind?

3. FOREVER FAMILY

All I wanted was to be liked. It never occurred to me to ask to be loved. Hell, I didn't even know what that was. All I wanted was a grown up to take my hand and say, "Come with me. I will be by your side. I will listen to you and play with you and tell you how truly wonderful you are." I was a 7 year-old girl holding out hope to find a friend. My brother, on the other hand, was his usual dreamy self, setting his sights too high for his own good. He told the social worker handling our case that he wanted a real mom and dad and a family where he could stay forever and ever. Ezra was like that. Even though he was two years older than me and should have known better, he didn't. I tried telling him that asking for a forever family was crazy but he shushed me with a wave of his hand.

Ezra turned to the social worker who was putting the six brown grocery bags containing our clothes and the three personal items we were allowed to take, into the trunk at the front of his baby blue Volkswagen Beetle car. Ezra asked, "What are my new mom and dad like?" and the social worker admitted he didn't know. He was just our driver for the trip from our foster home in Portland to our second chance at happiness in Eugene, Oregon.

After we climbed into the tiny backseat of his Beetle and the car pulled into the street, Ezra and I knelt together on the seat facing backwards, taking a last look at the home we'd known all our lives. We waved to the remaining unlucky foster kids who lined the curb in front of the big, two story house I thought we would never leave.

As we turned the corner and the view of the foster home was gone, the social worker told us to turn around, put on our seat belts and be quiet. He cranked up the radio's 1975 pop music, drowning us out and I thought "You are mean. I don't like you." I curled up on my half of the seat, promptly falling asleep from the overwhelming feelings of fear, excitement and confused longing that were pulsing through my body like stampeding horses. I slept without moving until we pulled into the driveway of our new home, our old life seemingly erased as easily as an incorrect math problem on a chalkboard.

I woke, pulling myself up and peeked through the front seats. The house was a single story ranch, with dark green siding. The house looked smaller and newer than our foster home. The grass was thick, with no dirt paths worn in the turf from kids riding bikes around the house. I spotted a dark-haired girl and blonde-haired boy about our ages racing to the front window and wondered who they were. I hoped they were temporary foster kids because then they wouldn't be competition for whatever attention the grown-ups might throw my way. I could handle temporary kids, there were a lot of them at the foster house.

We got out of the social worker's car and he handed each of us a bag of our clothes. A tall man called out a greeting from the front stoop as we approached, motioning to us to come inside. The social worker shook hands with adults while I shyly eyed the other boy and girl. I saw they were wearing nice dress clothes. They were not temporary, no foster kid would dress up to meet their competition. I never did.

Ezra and I were introduced to our new family, consisting of Harley and Virginia Spencer, their previously adopted children Matthew and Emelia, and Grandma Quigley, Virginia's mother. Harley was in his late 40's with a balding head and glasses. Virginia and Grandma Quigley wore shapeless house dresses that hid their lumpiness but their double chins gave their weight away. Matthew was close to Ezra's age and sported a funny bowl shaped haircut that I would recognize later on one of the Three Stooges. Matthew smiled a quirky kind of grimace at Ezra and me when prompted by Virginia. He then focused back on a large pink eraser he was carving into an intricately detailed sports car. Virginia told us Matthew used to have autism but he outgrew it. The social worker beamed and complimented Virginia on how well Matthew was doing. I didn't know what autism was, but Matthew seemed weird to me and I hoped I wouldn't catch it. After a flurry of happy noises the social worker dumped Ezra and me and our grocery sacks of clothes in the Spencer's house and he was gone. We were utterly on our own with strangers I was supposed to call my family. I was scared out of my mind. Ezra seemed ecstatic, smiling and hopping around, ready to begin his life with his forever family.

Emelia led me to our bedroom and asked how old I was. "I'm seven." I replied, wondering which of us was older. She said she was seven too. After doing the math we discovered I was six months older than her. I was also a grade ahead of her in school. In the fall I would start third grade in my new school and she would be in second grade. I was relieved we wouldn't be in the same grade. Emelia let me know that even though I was six months older and a grade ahead of her in school, she was adopted first so that meant she was number one. She was obviously Virginia's favorite, and looking at her it wasn't hard to see why. Emelia was a beautiful child. She had luxurious dark hair that naturally fell into loose ringlets. Her large dark eyes and long eyelashes were stunning. Her clear olive skin and even white teeth made her look like a perfect porcelain doll.

I, on the other hand, looked like a child raised by wolves. My thin, fine hair hung straight down like limp angel hair pasta. I was scrawny and always looked unwashed even if I had just bathed. My smile was a Howdy-Doody grin because of the gap in between my front teeth. The dentist told my foster mother I got the gap from sucking my thumb while I slept, which I needed to do if I wanted to fall asleep. No amount of yucky Thum, guaranteed to stop thumb sucking, painted on my digit was going to break my nighttime habit.

The morning after we arrived, Ezra and I were shown the washing machine and how to use it. I had to use a step stool to reach the knobs. We were expected to do our own laundry and we were given our chore assignments for the week. We four children did all the housework, except for grocery shopping and cooking. Grandma Quigley did that.

I was confused by Grandma Quigley. The first day I met her she had big, poufy snow-white hair and the next day, her hair was brownish, thin and barely covered her skull. I assumed there were two Grandma Quigley's because she looked so different. After a few days of me not being sure who was who, I noticed a head bust in Grandma's room that held her big hairdo. The mystery was solved when scraggly brown haired Grandma explained what a wig was. To this day, I think wigs are creepy.

We had no real chores while in the foster home, so Virginia had to give Ezra and I lessons on the proper way to vacuum, how to hold a rag to clean- not just smear dirt, how to scrub the bathtub and mop the floors. There were proper ways to fold towels, sweep the floor, wash windows, and wipe floorboards. Virginia sat in her recliner and supervised which ever unlucky kid was assigned a job within her view. I had no idea there were so many rules about cleaning and found Virginia's constant correction so maddening I just wanted to shout, "If you don't like how I'm doing it, why don't you get off your fat butt and do it yourself!" Of course, I didn't say that. Instead, I meekly bowed my head and finished my assigned chores as fast as possible. The sooner I got away from Virginia, the better. When I asked for an adult who would pay attention to me, she wasn't what I had in mind.

The only rooms in the house we kids didn't have to clean were Grandma Quigley's room, which was neat as a pin and Harley and Virginia's master bedroom and bathroom. We weren't allowed to enter their room unless we were invited in, which was rare. It was a good thing too. The first time I went into their darkly lit bedroom, I had to work to keep my face neutral, not registering my shock at the heaps of clothes and shoes and junk stacked in piles all over the room. The carpet had dark trails of dirt stain indicating their foot paths through the mess. Their bathroom was disgusting. The white sink was ringed with black, the mirror distorted with oily fingerprints and sprayed toothpaste. The toilet bowl was crusted with a permanent yellow stain. I couldn't believe that the same people that required perfection in the rest of the house could live like such pigs in their own room. No room in the foster home or at Ralph and Claudia's house ever looked as nasty as Harley and Virginia's bedroom. It looked like most of the mess was Virginia's stuff, but I didn't have time evaluate. I was invited in long enough to remove dirty dishes that were growing mold and stinking, so I was moving fast.

Emelia and I shared a bedroom literally out of the JCPenney Catalog. When Virginia found out Ezra and I were coming, she ordered new furniture for both the boys and girls rooms. Virginia showed me the pages in the catalog, pointing out the prices for each dresser, bed and linens so I could appreciate how much money was spent on our arrival.

"See that? Because it's printed in red, that means the sheets were on sale. But only the sheets. Everything else was full price. No expense was spared to give you girls the dream bedroom I would have loved to have when I was your age. Even now, my room isn't as nice as yours. I expect you to take care of it."

Our JCPenney bedroom consisted of two twin beds with overhead canopies, each with matching bed skirts, bed spreads, canopy tops and curtains for the windows. The pearlized white nightstands and dressers had edges painted in faux gold leaf. Virginia said, "You will make your bed every morning, then put the bedspread on over your blankets, then put the plain pillow on the bottom with this decorative pillow on top," as she waved a frilly pillow at Emelia and me. Virginia continued, "Weekly you will wipe down the wood frame and the top of your canopy so it doesn't collect dust. Right now the colors are yellow and white for summer but come next month we will change the linens to the winter patterns of brown, gold and white on the curtains, canopies, bedspreads and pillows."

I looked around and felt like I wasn't in my bedroom, but instead in a prop in a store front window, designed to sell the dream of luxurious living. I had no experience with maintaining this level of glamour and wasn't interesting in learning it.

During her regular inspections of our room Virginia pointed out my mistakes by using a yardstick to gesture, "Straighten that pillow. It belongs directly over the plain pillow. I shouldn't be able to see the under pillow. Pull the canopy top this way. It's crooked. This bottom part of your bed is lumpy. Remake it and pull the sheets tighter."

If I had too many things wrong with my side of the room, I got a lecture on how expensive it all was and how ungrateful I was acting. Her speeches would always end with a reminder of how she grew up dirt poor and how lucky I was to have such beautiful things.

In the foster home all the children slept on old metal army cots with just a single sheet and blanket or my favorite, sleeping bags. What could be more simple and to the point than a sleeping bag? There were no extra frills to pay attention to and there was no worry of anything breaking or getting dirty. No one got in trouble for having crooked pillows, either.

On our first Sunday with our adopted family, Virginia sent me to get dressed for church. She said, "Put on a dress and be sure to change out of your boots," pointing to my ever present blue suede ankle-high hiking boots.

"I don't have any dresses," I said.

Virginia sighed. "Fine. Have Emelia give you one of hers."

When I went to the closet to pick out a dress, Emelia flew to my side. "What are you doing?" she demanded.

I replied, "Virginia said I am supposed to wear one of your dresses."

"Well...you can't wear just anything. I will pick it out for you," Emelia said.

"Fine," I said, not caring a bit what I wore.

As I watched Emelia deliberate over her closet full of clothes, I marveled behind her shoulder. I didn't know anyone who had the same dress in three different colors. I didn't know anyone who had a closet, either. It was weird having a closet. The foster home was old enough the bedrooms didn't have closets, everyone's clothes were stored in the basement laundry room.

Emelia gave me a brown dress that she also had in dark blue and red. I preferred the blue but intuitively knew to not say anything. Emelia didn't want to share at all, but Virginia told her to quit fussing and let me have one dress until we could go shopping for proper clothes. Proper clothes? What was wrong with my clothes? I loved my clothes. I proudly dressed myself, thanks to the matching system built into all my Garanimal brand clothes. The shirts and pants were made for fool-proof matching by looking at the tags. Each tag had an animal on it. All I had to do was match a monkey shirt with a monkey pair of pants and I was guaranteed to look good. I took great pride in being able to dress myself from a young age because even I could match a giraffe to a giraffe, not a giraffe to a lion. So simple and yet so smart. At the Spencer's, my clothes weren't up to snuff. It wasn't long before I was given a wardrobe makeover and my Garanimals were no more. They were replaced by random clothes that had no system to them. I was doomed to Emelia and Virginia telling me when something didn't match. I resented having to change my clothes several times until I found an outfit acceptable to Virginia. It was especially hard to get used to dressing up for church services when I never had to before. The churches I attended at the foster home and with my real parents didn't require the same level of formality that our adoptive God did. My favorite shoes were my blue suede hiking boots lined with red fabric. I called them waffle stompers because the square tread pattern on the bottom of the sole looked just like waffles. I wore them everywhere, including church. Our adoptive God, however, expected shiny dress shoes that pinched my toes and made me walk with smaller steps to avoid blisters. I was off to a rocky start with this God. So far, I wasn't seeing how His plan was working out in my favor.

One Sunday Virginia had to be to church early so Harley brought us kids separately in his car so we wouldn't have to sit around an extra hour before services began. As we filed into the chapel and squeezed past Virginia in the pew, I heard her stage whisper to Harley, "What the hell is Haddie wearing? Where did she find that ridiculous outfit?"

Harley shrugged and said "She looks fine. No one is going to care."

Virginia hissed back, "I swear she does this on purpose. She deliberately picks clothes that make her look like a clown just to make me look bad."

My face burned with shame as I angrily thought, "I picked a dress you bought and white tights you insisted I wear just last month!"

Until Virginia's comment, I was proud of my outfit and thought I looked really cute. Now I was reduced to sitting squished in a chapel pew with a family I didn't want, singing an opening hymn about how wonderful it was to be part of a happy eternal family. I hated all of it.

Ezra proclaimed he was happy to have a family of his very own and he set about trying to win their love. At first, announcing he wanted a hug and kiss, Ezra ran across the room full steam, smack into whichever adult he targeted. He grabbed them in a bear hug and kissed them so hard he loosened their dentures. After a few days of stunned politeness, Virginia forbade Ezra's 'Launches for Love' on the grounds it could hurt Grandma Quigley. The adults seemed to breathe a sigh of relief.

I didn't offer to hug and kiss them. I had lived in a foster home for six years where I was never hugged or kissed by my foster parents and the only intimate contact I had I didn't want, so I was definitely not seeking physical affection.

Ezra was excited about having his own family, one that wouldn't be mean but would love him. He yearned to belong so badly. I didn't feel like I needed another family. I wanted love and attention just as much as my brother but I didn't want another family. It was hard enough strategizing in our old situation, constantly monitoring the moods of grownups, looking for signs of possible trouble. Now we were starting all over, with new people with unknown motives, where we were definitely the outsiders.

Within a few weeks of being with the Spencers I told Virginia my biggest secret. While she supervised me washing dishes by hand because the dishwasher didn't do a good enough job, I tentatively asked, "What would you think if I told you in the foster home I was in a secret club?"

Virginia breezily replied, "Oh really? What kind of club?"

I took a deep breath and told her that while I was in the foster home, I was part of a club my older foster brothers made and that we played Naked Games. Virginia listened, her mouth hard around the edges. She handed me a dish towel to wipe the glasses and matter-of-factly said, "That's over now, so you don't need to talk about it."

She didn't say anything else to me and I finished the dishes in silence. The next afternoon I overheard her telling Grandma Quigley she thought I told her a story to get sympathy. I was crushed and humiliated. I thought my new family was supposed to love me and care about me. Who would admit to such an embarrassing thing just for attention? I had hoped Virginia would comfort and reassure me that would never happen again, but her response told me otherwise. I thought, "You just flunked your test. I will never trust you with anything."

The Spencers had a ritual of kneeling in a big circle while holding hands for family prayer before bedtime. Virginia and Grandma Quigley couldn't kneel because they were too heavy, so they leaned forward in their recliners to hold hands within the circle. Virginia liked to offer long-winded prayers that would go on and on, listing the faults of each child and asking God to help them overcome their weaknesses. My consistent sins were being too secretive and not being loving to the adults. I didn't tell Virginia what I thought about things and only answered her prying questions with non-committal yes's and no's. As for not being loving, besides the fact I wasn't even sure what healthy physical affection was, these people were total strangers to me. Just because I got dumped on their doorstep and the grown-ups decided this was my family, didn't mean I would magically fall in love. As I settled into the routine of expecting fifteen minute long prayers, I blocked out Virginia's voice in my ears and focused on finding the most comfortable positions on the braided floor rug to rest my sore knees. I floated away in my mind to a happy place, usually climbing trees. I always came back to the ground with a thump when my brain registered hearing, "Amen."

Following family prayer the kids were expected to kiss the adults before bedtime. On one occasion at the end of family prayer, I was unable to escape to the bathroom in time and was forced to line up with the other children. I kissed Harley, then Grandma Quigley and waited my turn for Virginia. She took longer because she grabbed each of us, kissed and hugged us and whispered something in our ear that required a response from the child. When it was my turn, she kissed me and whispered in my ear, "That was a Judas kiss and I know it."

I didn't know how to respond so I pulled back and stood in front of her chair. Virginia didn't let my silence go. She pressed, this time aloud so everyone could hear, "Do you know what a Judas kiss is?"

I admitted I didn't. In all my years of suffering through church meetings with my real parents and the occasional Bible class from neighborhood churches with the other foster children I had never heard of Judas. I had heard the Noah and the Ark story. Over and over, no matter what church I went to, every church favored Noah and his Ark for children's services. Judas however, was new to me. Virginia launched into how Judas deceived Christ and how with his kiss he sealed Jesus's fate on the cross. Judas killed Jesus. So a Judas kiss was not a kiss of love. That story really hurt my tender seven year-old feelings. Although I didn't have loving feelings for Virginia, Harley or Grandma Quigley and they had yet to win my trust, I still was offended that Virginia would say I was like Judas. All I wanted in the whole world was to be loved. Was I as terrible as Judas? I didn't think so.

Actually, I thought I was a pretty good kid. I was getting the hang of doing the house work to Virginia's satisfaction and my life-long survival skill of being outside as much as possible was serving me well. As soon as my daily chores were done, I was outside roaming the neighborhood as late as I could.

Things in our forever family were not turning out the way my brother had hoped. Where I was feeling unappreciated and as lonely as ever, Ezra was in the boot camp of his life. The social workers told the Spencers when we were adopted that he was 'slow.' Since Virginia had done such a fine job curing Matthew of autism, the state workers thought she would be perfect for Ezra. He got easily frustrated and threw temper tantrums. That behavior isn't unusual in a two year-old but is noticeable in a nine year-old.

Ezra was a late bloomer in every way, including toilet training. His poor toileting habits became such an offensive trigger for adults that I knew to be careful to never ever, have an accident in my bed or pants. I saw what happened to my brother when he did.

While camping with our foster family, Ezra pooped in his pants and Wayne lost it. He yelled at Ezra, grabbed him by the shoulder and marched him down to a nearby stream. I could clearly hear Ezra's screams as he was spanked. Then I heard splashing as Ezra's clothes were stripped off and he was forcibly washed in the freezing water. As he dragged Ezra shivering back to our campsite, Wayne announced since my brother was too lazy to go to the bathroom, he could wear it instead. He forced Ezra's dirty underwear around his neck, putting his head thru the leg holes, so as he said, "Ezra could smell his own shit."

I was shocked into silence.

It didn't take long for Ezra's chronic bladder and bowel problems to appear with a vengeance at the Spencers. He wet the bed every night and seemed to be unable to sense when he needed to use the bathroom during the day. Despite raising six other children before us, Harley and Virginia had no idea how to handle it. Ezra didn't automatically wash his dirty sheets, or change his clothes. He didn't bathe unless he was told to, and even then he might not use soap. Ezra peed his pants daily and at least once a week pooped in them. He was oblivious to the smell and seemed sincerely surprised when he was told to change his clothes.

Ezra wanted to be included in games and activities, but was always out of step with the group. Spending his early years in front of the tv at the foster home didn't serve him well in learning social skills. He couldn't follow jokes or conversations and his random, pointless comments fell flat. He especially had a hard time at the Spencers because we children were not given control of the tv, the one thing in the foster home he did have free reign of. In the foster home Ezra didn't go outside to play. He preferred to spend his time in front of the small black and white tv, watching hours of Sesame Street, Batman, cartoons and whatever else was on the three network channels. If forced outside, he would stand at the door, wailing and pounding on the glass to be let back in. His old ways of handling frustration by crying and throwing temper tantrums ceased at the Spencers the first time he was beaten with a belt. This same punishment, no matter how often repeated, did not have the same result on his bladder and bowel control.

The Spencers were big fans of a popular book, "Dare to Discipline" by Dr. James Dobson which advocated a no-nonsense, corporal punishment approach to parenting. The regular punishment for any child whose chores were not done to Virginia's satisfaction was no dinner. I was stunned the first time Ezra didn't get to eat dinner. The next day I tried to help him with his chores. Virginia saw that I was helping Ezra and she kept me busy doing things for her so there was no time to help him before the 4 p.m. cutoff for chore completion. Ezra went another night with no supper. It wasn't that Ezra was disobedient. He started a job like cleaning the bathroom and two hours later with the bathtub full of water, he was engrossed in playing with Matthew's Navy Seal G.I. Joe men, having completely forgotten he had work to do. It happened over and over and the punishment never changed.

When Ezra did earn the right to eat with the family, he refined a habit of wolfing down his food. In the foster home Ezra and I both learned to eat as fast as possible because if we didn't, there was a good chance the food would be gone. Our foster mother served food in big bowls and platters in the middle of the table and it was a free-for-all to grab your share. One morning she made pancakes for breakfast and I didn't move fast enough. All the other kids took the hotcakes from the platter before I could get one. When I complained to Dorothy, she tipped up the empty batter bowl and said, "Sorry. There is none left. I guess you can make yourself a piece of toast."

At the Spencers Ezra not only ate as much as possible, he squirreled away food in his cheeks and only emptied them if Virginia demanded he swallow what was in his mouth. It was obvious he was eating as much as possible to store up for the unknown stretch of time until his next meal.

I didn't miss many meals at the Spencer's for not getting my jobs done. Instead, I wasn't allowed to eat dinner because I rushed and didn't do a thorough enough job. Dishes weren't dry enough or I missed a spot in vacuuming. I was also forbidden to eat dinner for other infractions like rolling my eyes or acting annoyed when given a command. During the summer not being allowed to eat dinner wasn't a problem for me because the neighborhood was full of cherry, apple and plum trees ripe for the picking. My expert tree climbing skills, honed during years of dodging trouble at the foster home, served me well. There were also wild blackberries, raspberries and honeysuckle plants to eat. Sometimes I ate so much fruit that I got the runs but it was worth it to be able to passive-aggressively thumb my nose at Virginia and her stupid rules.

Since the state workers told Harley and Virginia that Ezra was slow, Virginia decided to have him tested. The results showed he was above average intelligence. The psychologist told her that Ezra was gifted in unusual ways and he would benefit from regular counseling to explore how he perceived the world.

Following the doctor's visit, Virginia came home and announced there was nothing at all wrong with Ezra. In her opinion he had been pulling the wool over their eyes. He wasn't slow at all. In fact, he was just the opposite. Instead of following the psychologist's advice to get counseling, she decided nothing was wrong with him and he was just being stubborn. In that minute, I knew Ezra's fate was sealed.

Virginia decided if Ezra didn't want to wash his sheets, he didn't need sheets or blankets. If he didn't care to do his chores the way she wanted them done, he was banished to his bedroom. He also wasn't allowed to be in the family room with everyone else because only people who worked got to watch tv. After school and chores he was sent straight to his bedroom, which was stripped bare of all toys, entertainment and comfort. Ezra had nothing on his side of the bedroom he shared with Matthew. He needed to earn the privilege of pillows, sheets, blankets, toys, paper, pens, everything. The only thing on his side of the room was a mattress encased in plastic and a bare dresser. Everything was taken away to force Ezra to follow the rules, do his chores and not to wet his bed or mess in his pants.

The main form of discipline used on us, besides missing dinner, was spankings with wooden spoons, sticks, belts and wooden boat oars. Virginia told us repeatedly how good we had it, compared to the beatings she got from Grandma Quigley as a child. I couldn't understand how creaky, slow-moving Grandma could have done the terrible things Virginia talked about, until I noticed her encouraging Virginia and Harley in doling out punishments. She caught me running in the house or turning on the tv without permission and wouldn't say a word. She waited until Harley got home and then ratted me out. Some days I swear she must have had a notebook hidden in her voluminous caftan to keep all our infractions fresh in her mind for reporting.

After one spanking Ezra called the police to complain of abuse. I was impressed that he had the courage to call 911. The police listened to his story and then talked to Harley and Virginia. The officers had Ezra pull his pants down and they took pictures of his backside. Unfortunately it wasn't one of the hard spankings, so all that showed on his skin was a few faded red streaks. The official police interview consisted of me, Matthew and Emelia lining up and saying in front of our parents that we were never spanked without deserving it and that it never left bruises. The policeman taking notes remarked to Harley and Virginia that they were wonderful people for adopting damaged kids and if Ezra was his kid he would have spanked him too. After the police left, Ezra was spanked again and sent to bed. I buried my head in my pillow to muffle his screams. I was angry and scared. I had no way to stop my brother's torture without getting hit myself and I was spanked enough to know I didn't want to get hit the way he was. I was terrified of the pain and ashamed I wasn't willing to suffer for him. The next day I couldn't look Ezra in the eyes because I felt so bad about my selfishness. The Spencers decided Ezra was incredibly stubborn, and it would just be a matter of time before his will would break. Only then could they train him properly to work and contribute to the family.

The truth was we were beaten excessively. It did leave welts and bruises. I came up with the idea of wearing three or four pairs of underwear when a spanking was coming. My technique, which I whispered to the others, didn't last long because we weren't yelling as much and Harley caught on. To make up for our deceit we were beaten bare bottomed occasionally, just to check that we weren't trying to pad ourselves.

Our neighbors were aware of the number of beatings at our house. In the summertime the windows were open and they could hear it. The retired couple next door asked me how many times we got spanked and what kinds of things got us into trouble. I answered their questions honestly, hoping they would report the Spencers for child abuse. I understood the complaint had to come from someone outside the family. No one would believe me, just like the police didn't believe my brother. Evidently the neighbor talked to Virginia because she informed me I wasn't allowed to talk to the neighbors anymore because "they are just a bunch of nosy people looking to have something to talk about." Since nothing came of my conversation with the neighbors, I decided Virginia was right, they were just being nosy and I gave up hoping they would save us.

Another punishment technique of the Spencers was called Compound Punishment. Emelia snuck into a box of Virginia's chocolates and ate ten pieces. When the missing candy was discovered she was forced to lie across a padded footstool and was hit with a stick ten times for each piece she took. Then, because she lied about eating the candy when she was first asked about it, her punishment was compounded. She was forced to eat the remaining five pounds of chocolates until she got sick and violently threw up. Compound Punishment went into effect for being caught in a lie, so I learned to be sneaky and not say much for fear of accidentally incriminating myself.

We children didn't get treats so I learned to limit myself to one or two forbidden potato chips. Always careful to not disturb packaging, I never ate anything lined up in rows where it would be obvious some was missing. I drank Virginia's flat, ice diluted soda leftovers, filched a few stale Doritos chips from her open bag or licked the wrapper left from an empty package of donuts while I cleaned around her chair.

Virginia turned her recliner into a throne, from which she ruled her kingdom. It was surrounded by stacks of magazines, mail, anything she might use within reach of her seat. Our job was to straighten the piles, daily clearing out any empty candy wrappers, dirty dishes and to retrieve the remote that often slid down the side of the chair cushions while she sat and watched tv. This was the most stressful chore in the house because if her chair wasn't done before she woke up at 4p.m. and if we were within her arm's length while we worked, she had no problem hitting us upside our heads if we made a mistake or weren't working fast enough to satisfy her.

The worst thing was when the TV remote was misplaced. Heaven help us all if the remote wasn't found instantly. With the way Virginia bellowed and screeched until it was found, you would have thought someone stole her baby. I lived in fear of that damn remote.

The other thing I dreaded was noon on Saturdays. Every Saturday at twelve noon, Harley or Virginia inspected our bedrooms. If they weren't clean, including all clothes washed, dried, folded and put neatly in our dresser drawers, we got an automatic spanking for not finishing our chores on time. Because of the clothes requirement, it wasn't enough to hurriedly clean on Saturday morning. For all four of us to have our clothes washed and dried before the deadline, we needed to coordinate the washing and drying through the week so we had enough time to get it done. We weren't allowed to have any clothes in either the washer or dryer by Saturday noon, the machines had to be clear of our clothes so Harley could wash his and Virginia's clothes on Saturday afternoons. Virginia didn't do laundry.

One Saturday, Emelia and I faced a mound of clothes on our bedroom floor. Half was clean, half was dirty and it was all mixed up. Since we were only six months apart in age, we wore the same size clothes and it was an ongoing, frustrating argument on who wore what and who was the slob of our room. During the week whatever clothes we tried on and didn't find suitable, we both wadded up and shoved into the back of our closet. Virginia didn't check the closet during the week and especially not the back because that would have required her to bend down and she didn't do that. If our shared hamper was full, dirty clothes also got added into the closet pile. It hadn't occurred to either of us to ask for another hamper so we each had our own. We assumed if Virginia wanted us to have individual hampers, she would have given them to us.

On Saturday Harley had been warning us all morning to hurry up and get our inside chores done because he wanted us to weed the large vegetable garden in the backyard. He wanted it done before the afternoon sun got too hot. With 45 minutes to go, he called from the front door, "I'm running to the hardware store. When I get back, your rooms better be done." When the door slammed behind him, the timer was set. Emelia and I faced off, accusing each other of not doing our fair share of the work. "This is the pink shirt you wore on Tuesday. You should have washed it," I said, while she thrust a pair of pants into my arms.

"Well, these are the jeans you tried on that didn't fit you. Put them away."

"I didn't try those on. I don't even like them," I replied. Around and around our circular, non-productive argument continued, until we both realized there was only 10 minutes left and that Harley would be back at any time. In a collective panic, we stopped arguing and furiously started folding. It wasn't going to work, there was too much to fold and put away. We were out of time. As our eyes both turned fearful and full of anticipatory tears, knowing Harley wouldn't hold back on our whippings, a brilliant thought streaked into my mind. Garbage bags! That would solve our problem. We could put the clothes in black plastic garbage bags, and then put them outside our bedroom window during inspection. After inspection, we could haul them back in before Harley went on that side of the house, which he rarely did. Emelia helped me stuff the clothes into two large black lawn and leaf bags. I went outside around the house and she lowered the bags down to me on the ground. It was going to work. Brilliant! With minutes to spare, we excitedly showed Matthew our solution to the problem of what to do with clothes. He seemed impressed. I offered that if he ever needed our window for his stuff he was welcome to it because he and Ezra's bedroom window over looked the back patio and anything out their window would be easily spotted.

We heard Harley's car pull up out front and everyone split, no one wanting to be near the garbage bags. The bags were shouting their accusations of deception so loudly in my ears I could hardly hear Harley as he entered the house and announced it was inspection time. He retrieved the Spanking Stick from its proper place behind the family room door and used it in Matthew and Ezra's room to lift blankets and move things in their closet, looking for evidence of misplaced items. The boys' room passed inspection as usual because Matthew was tidy to a fault and Ezra had nothing to be messed up. When Harley came to our room, Emelia and I both casually draped ourselves near the window, attempting to block any stray thoughts of looking outside. As he poked under our beds with his stick and opened our dresser drawers, Harley begrudgingly complimented us on our cooperation in getting our room done so efficiently. As he stepped out our doorway, he commented, "See what happens when you work together? You get the job done. Looks good, no spankings today."

Emelia and I exchanged sly smiles of relief.

Harley didn't even get ten feet away from our doorway when Matthew's inbred inability to live with a lie kicked in. My body drained all color in one giant whoosh as Matthew led Harley back into our bedroom and pointed out the garbage bags outside our window. Emelia and I both burst into tears, sobbing as we realized what was coming. A spanking for not getting our room clean and a Compound Punishment for our attempt to hide the evidence. I don't remember the details of our punishment. Thankfully my mind has carried that trauma away from my awareness, freeing me from the memories.

We kids were told to be grateful for the food we got because they didn't have to adopt us. Occasionally a pie or tray of pastries would turn bad before Virginia had a chance to eat it. She left it on the kitchen counter, announcing we were free to have it. In the beginning I scraped off the mold and ate the dessert. After a while my resentment grew and I refused to eat rotten food. I decided Virginia was a slothful cow who complained about her ill health but never got off her butt. If it wasn't for crotchety old Grandma Quigley doing the cooking, we kids would have never been fed.

Six months into our placement with the Spencers, a social worker I vaguely remembered from the foster home, came and interviewed Ezra and me. She talked to us in the living room, a place we weren't allowed to enter without permission unless we were dusting or vacuuming. After Virginia nodded her head, we kids all sat on the couch my butt hadn't touched since the day my brother and I moved in. With the whole family present, the social worker complimented the Spencers on their comfortable home and told Ezra and me we were lucky to have such a nice family. Not many older children were adopted, especially not together. We definitely had a lot to be grateful for.

I wanted to ask questions, like "How are the foster kids doing without us? Do Claudia and Ralph have our new phone number and address? Are Claudia and Ralph going to visit us in our new house?"

I was afraid to get into trouble with our new parents, so I didn't ask anything. I sat quietly and smiled during our final interview with the state social worker.

I didn't realize we had not yet been adopted. I thought it was over the day we arrived at the Spencers. I was wrong. Months later, our certificates of adoption arrived in the mail. Virginia sat Ezra and I down in the living room and showed us the documents. She said, "Now you are officially ours. We are a family and no one can take you away."

She was smiling and hugged us. Ezra also seemed pleased. I was not pleased, not at all. I thought, "Wait a minute. All this time we have lived with you and you weren't our parents?" I realized I had missed a window of opportunity to get out of this mess and now it was too late. I was really stuck.

How in the hell did I end up here, anyway? I didn't know the details of my life. When you are a foster kid, adults whisper to each other about you. No one openly tells funny stories of the first time you tasted a sour pickle in your highchair or how you smiled your first smile and farted at exactly the same time so your parents argued for days over whether it really was a smile or just a case of bad gas. Those kinds of stories are private, inside comforts reserved only for lucky children who have been told their pasts and who look to the same adults to guide their futures. My brother and I had neither. We didn't know our past, the present made no sense, and the future loomed like a black hole of nothingness. We were not lucky children and I didn't know why.

Virginia asked Ezra and me if we wanted to change our first names, since our last names were changing with the adoption. My ears perked up; I was definitely interested since I had hated my name. I am told Hadassah is a common girl's name in Jewish communities, but we weren't Jewish. My distaste for my name only grew as I became school age. Struggling to print H-A-D-A-S-S-A-H in kindergarten guaranteed I missed out on precious recess time because I couldn't write my name as fast as girls lucky enough to be named Ann or June. Besides, anyone who has ever been a child on a playground would know a name that has ASS in the middle of it is like having a permanent bull's-eye target on your back.

My nickname and what I insisted on being called, was Haddie. I still got grief, "Haddie, Haddie 2 x 4, couldn't fit through a kitchen door," was the taunt I heard on the playground, which was stupid because I was far from being unable to fit through a door. I was a scrawny kid who needed a belt to hold up my jeans. That ticked me off too, but was still better than being called Hud-ASS-uh while kids ran around me, braying like donkeys.

Ezra wasn't so sure about changing his first name. He liked his name and the honor behind it. I couldn't have cared less about the honor of my name. All it brought me was trouble and I was ready to dump it.

The Spencers liked the idea of us completely changing our names and making a fresh start. Virginia handed a piece of paper to each of us saying, "I took the liberty to write down a list of first names that I think sound nice with the last name Spencer. You look them over and decide which you would like. It is your decision to make."

Ezra studied his list and asked about each name, wanting to know if they had any meaning to them. He picked "Rex" as his new first name, because it means King. He decided to keep Ezra as his middle name because he wanted the honor of that Old Testament name. I looked at my list and couldn't read Virginia's fancy handwriting. I was too embarrassed to admit I couldn't read cursive letters so I went with what looked prettiest to me. When Virginia read aloud the names I picked, Maria Heather I liked them well enough to keep them. I didn't ask to hear any other names. After I said I wanted Maria Heather, Virginia asked, "Are you sure? I really hoped you would like the name at the top. It is my favorite name for you."

I didn't say anything in reply. I couldn't because I didn't know what the name at the top was. Grandma Quigley, who was sitting nearby asked, "Virginia, what name did you like?"

Virginia turned to her and said, "Maria Laina. Isn't that pretty? I really like it. Maria Laina would fit Haddie so well."

I immediately stiffened. I couldn't have hated Maria Laina more than I did in that instant. I wasn't going to dump Haddassah just to be saddled with a weird name like Maria Laina. What was wrong with her? I looked down at the table and said quietly I preferred to keep the names I picked out. Virginia started to reply back but Harley cut her off, reminding her she said it was our choice what our new names would be. I was grateful for his intervention. I didn't know if I was strong enough to go up against her if she made a big deal about Maria Laina but I really, really didn't want that as my new name. After a day or two, before Virginia finished the paperwork, I decided I liked Heather better so I asked her to flip the names and Maria became my new middle name. My birth name, Hadassah Clinton Contrella Wade had no meaning to me. I didn't feel I was turning my back on Ralph and Claudia by getting rid of it. All I was doing was lessening the chance I would be teased at school. I wanted to be a normal kid like everyone else, not a girl with a funny name.

I clung to my beloved keepsakes from my early foster life. I read and reread the pages of the storybook Bedknobs and Broomsticks, remembering the voice of Angela Lansbury as it chirped through the record player speakers at the foster home. I didn't dare ask to listen to my record at the Spencers. At their house the record player was like the radio, microwave and tv, all off limits to children without adult permission and I didn't see that ever changing.

The only toy I had brought from Portland, my Mrs. Beasley doll, was my greatest comfort. I slept with her and proudly pulled her voice box string whenever someone inquired about my ever-present doll. One day we had visitors at the Spencers, a seemly rare occasion compared the rowdy door-slamming parade of stomping feet that invaded the foster home. It was a mother with her three little kids over to discuss church music with Virginia. My job was to entertain the three children so Virginia and their mother could do their business without interruption. The smallest girl glommed onto my Mrs. Beasley doll and I reluctantly let her play with it to keep her quiet. At the end of the visit, the little girl wouldn't give back my doll. When I tried to take it from her, she wailed and big tears ran down her chubby cheeks. Her mother looked apologetically at Virginia and explained something about how the little girl had been having a hard time lately due to blah, blah, blah. I didn't care what the girl's problem was, I wanted my doll back. It was the only doll I'd ever had as my own. I had to give up my Barbie's and all the other toys Santa had brought me when I went to the Spencers and I wasn't about to see my Mrs. Beasley doll go away. That was my position until Virginia used a warning tone of voice I already recognized as dangerous as she said, "Let the baby have the doll. I'll get you another one just like it."

I looked at her and tears filled my eyes. "But it's mine," I whispered. "It's my Mrs. Beasley. I want to keep it."

Virginia said to me, "Don't be silly. You are too old for

dolls and you don't need it. Jesus expects you to share with others and don't you think He would be very happy if you did the right thing and shared your doll?" Virginia turned to the mother and said, "Don't worry. She can have it. I'll buy her a new one. It's no problem."

Virginia gently pushed them towards the open door, shooing them onto the stoop. As they departed across the front lawn, I caught a glimpse of my favorite doll as it left my life, just like everything else I owned. After the door was firmly shut Virginia sighed and murmured to herself, "That was torture. Won't be doing that again."

She shuffled out of the formal living room and planted herself in her recliner throne in the family room. No mention was made of my Mrs. Beasley and I never got another one.

Within a few months of living with the Spencers my confidence in my ability to protect my brother was broken. The Spencers were bigger and meaner than the adults at the foster home.

The first time I tried to step in to save Rex from a spanking, Virginia said justice demanded punishment – would I be willing to take Rex's punishment for him? I couldn't believe that she really meant it until I tested her by nodding yes, I would take my brother's punishment. She looked straight into my eyes and said, "Fine. You can take Rex's spanking. Harley, go get the stick."

I lay across the green vinyl footstool as I received ten whacks with the hard wood stick to teach Rex to do his assigned work. I didn't hold back my screams. I wanted them to feel badly for what they did to me. It had no effect on them other than Virginia turned to Rex, who they forced to watch, and said, "I hope you are ashamed your sister took your punishment."

Rex looked at the floor, his face not registering any emotion. After that, I realized Harley and Virginia had no limits. There was no way to protect him without putting myself directly in the Spencer's crosshairs. I couldn't do it. I couldn't put my fear aside to help my brother.

As the harsh realities of our adoptive life unfolded, I clung to my memories of our foster home and our real parents to give me comfort and courage. All I had to do was survive the Spencers house until I could figure out how to get back to our old life, which I didn't realize until then, I missed terribly.

4. HAPPILY EVER AFTER

When Rex and I moved to our adopted home in Eugene, more than our address and names changed. Instead of attending Buckman Elementary, a two-story urban school covered with graffiti painted on its red brick wall, we were now enrolled at Fairfield Elementary, a small one-story school with white middle-class students and teachers. I was in third grade and nervous, worried I wouldn't find a teacher who would like me. For the first few weeks of school, my anxiety was made worse. Virginia got up with us kids in the morning, made breakfast and packed our lunches. It should have been a comforting gesture, but Virginia was so incredibly grumpy in the morning that I dreaded leaving my bedroom. She made me go back and change my clothes if she didn't like what I was wearing or how I combed my hair. She barked orders about sitting up straight and finishing every bite of our oatmeal. I wasn't used to being micromanaged. The foster home was 'every man for himself' and I liked that freedom. My new adoptive parents, especially Virginia, stressed me. I never knew if she was going to be nice and complimentary or gripe about my ungratefulness and slothfulness. At least in the foster home Dorothy was predictable in her neglect. She never berated me about not cleaning up or said I was lazy. I wasn't used to being criticized like this and longed to be ignored.

Luckily it didn't take long for Virginia to revert back to her normal habit of staying up late watching tv until 4 a.m. Harley would leave for work by 6:45a.m. I waited until he was gone and then I got up in peace. I was usually out of the house no later than 7:10 a.m. with my self- packed peanut butter and jelly sandwich and a piece of fruit.

I stopped taking the bus since it arrived in our neighborhood at 7:45a.m. and was full of kids who picked on Rex and whoever was with him. Instead, I walked or rode my bike to my new friend Leslie's house. She and I met in our first weeks of school. She was kind and made me feel included. For the first time in my life, it didn't matter as much if I had a teacher as my ally because I had my first real friend. I pretended I had always been a nice girl, hoping I would get the chance to be accepted as a regular kid. I sat in Leslie's kitchen talking to her mother while she got ready.

Leslie's mom was pleasant in the morning and never acted like it was weird I showed up so early on their doorstep, sometimes even before Leslie was out of bed. She didn't let on it was a problem; although there were a couple of times I had to wait outside until she woke up and sleepily let me in while she poured herself a cup of coffee. Leslie was a nice girl, from a nice family. Before her I was never allowed to play in a nice family's house. I was the 'bad influence' while in foster care. Leslie was impressed when I showed her the scar on my forearm from an immunization and told her it was a scar from a stabbing.

Leslie's mom fascinated me. Her stylishly short jet-black hair was cut in a wavy bob. She wore well-fitting clothes that showed her figure. I secretly fantasized hugging her and just knew that if I did, my arms would reach all the way around, unlike Virginia and Grandma Quigley. I also dreamt that if I hugged her, she would hug me back. She talked to me and treated me like I was normal. She was a good seamstress and made Leslie's shirts and jeans. I thought that was so cool. I wanted a mother like her. On the rare occasion Leslie would complain about her folks I couldn't understand. In my eyes they were perfect. I pretended I wasn't just walking Leslie to school, but instead we were sisters who were best friends and we were leaving our house together in the morning. What a wonderful fantasy that was.

In the 4th grade, my PE class had a swimming unit. As I was dressing in the girl's locker room our classroom teacher, Mrs. Koffler, noticed Sidney, the girl next to me, had bruises on her legs. She asked where the bruises came from and Sidney told her it was an accident. Mrs. Koffler kept asking questions as Sidney dressed and then took her away. The next day Mrs. Koffler announced Sidney wouldn't be coming back to our class. I knew what happened without anyone telling me. I half wished I had bruises so Rex and I could be taken away from the Spencers, but what good would that do? We'd just end up back in foster care, where more abuse and maybe even worse stuff could happen. I was still trying to figure out how to manage Virginia and Harley.

The first time I experienced rage, not just anger, but full-on rage, was when I was ten years-old. I didn't know until then how it felt to be so full of adrenaline that doing superhuman feats of strength like, The Incredible Hulk, were possible.

I was washing dishes after supper in the kitchen when Virginia called Rex's name. He didn't respond since his bedroom door was shut, as usual. I went to his door and cracked it open. Rex was lying on the bed, reading a smuggled comic book. As I opened the door he slid the comic under his stained mattress. He raised his head and looked up at me. "Mom wants you," I said.

"For what?" he asked. I shrugged I don't know. I went back to the kitchen and began washing again, this time slower so I could hear what was happening in the family room. Virginia asked Rex if he vandalized her furniture. He was confused by the question and couldn't answer directly. She told him to go back to his room, look at the front panel on his dresser and see if his name was scratched on it. He did as he was told. He went back to Virginia and said that his name was scraped on it with a straight pin, but it didn't hurt the wood, it just took the paint off. Virginia asked, "Is it your dresser? Did you have permission to write your name on my dresser?" This was bad. This was so, so bad. Rex was really going to get beat for this.

I tensed up, waiting for what was coming. Virginia said, "Since you like to put your name on stuff that doesn't belong to you, I am going to tattoo my name on your butt to help you remember."

She told Rex to go to the kitchen and get the package of food coloring dye used to color Easter eggs. He came into the kitchen where I was standing in horrified silence, feeling completely helpless. I whispered to him to run away. Just leave. I was terrified, convinced she would really do it. He hesitated and I kept telling him to just run out the side door before it was too late. Virginia called from the family room, telling him to quit stalling and get back in there with the dye. What could I do to protect my brother? My mind was filled with nothing but the impulse to run. Run! Run! Run! Get the hell away from here!

Rex sighed and went back to her in the family room. She burned the end of a sewing needle with a match, explaining to him that it would make the needle sterile. Then she told him to take down his pants and underwear and lean across her lap. He complied.

My insides howled with rage. I hated Virginia with all my guts. I washed the dishes silently, my hands shaking with adrenaline and emotion. I wanted to smash the kitchen counters, rip down the cupboards over my head, and strangle Virginia with my bare hands. I listened intently to every noise from the family room, vowing to tell what happened the next day at school. Now we would have proof of abuse. But after making a big deal of deciding how big the letters should be, and what color the letters should be, toying with my brother like a cat teasing a mouse, Virginia finally let him up without touching him with the needle and told him to never carve his name on her furniture ever again. I was shaking from fear, relief, and hate.

Harley and Grandma Quigley just sat and watched the

whole thing, not intervening at all. Rex was 12 years-old. I remember his age only because the next day Virginia told Grandma how shocked she was at how underdeveloped his sexual organs were, considering his age. Grandma Quigley agreed that she too, was surprised at the appearance of his genitals. I was cleaning in the same room and was humiliated at the way they were talking about my brother. They were either oblivious to my presence or didn't care.

I hated Virginia for being so cruel. I had no feelings of gratitude or love for her. I didn't know what the social workers were talking about, telling me that we were lucky to be with the Spencers. I felt like the child in the fable "The Emperor's New Clothes." Was I the only one who could see how they were?

I couldn't understand why the Spencers adopted children when they treated us so badly. The only reason that came to my mind was they got us to work around the house. When I was in 4th grade history class we learned about slavery in America. I understood the concept. I felt like a slave bought only to serve my masters. I couldn't see any honorable reason for the Spencers to have adopted us.

On tv there were a lot of promotions for an upcoming documentary special about a family called the DeBolts. Virginia was really excited about watching it and she made a point to write the tv show date and time on the calendar in the kitchen. When it came on the whole family was summoned, including Ezra from his bedroom, to watch it.

The DeBolts were a couple who adopted nineteen disabled children. As we watched the show I looked for signs of wrong doing and abuse. In my mind, there was no way this couple could have taken in that many kids with so many physical and mental problems. Did they do it for the money, like my foster parents? Did they do it so others would think they were wonderful people, like I assumed the Spencers did? How much of the daily work was done by the parents and how much by the kids? I watched Virginia out of the corner of my eye as the show progressed, wondering what she was thinking. Was this inspiring her to adopt even more kids? Did she want to adopt a child with disabilities? Why was she so interested in the DeBolts? Did she compare herself to them?

When the show ended, I was relieved. There were no signs of harsh treatment of the DeBolt children that I could see from the film, but I still had my doubts about their motives. I did not walk away from it the way Virginia and Harley did, saying that it was inspirational and encouraging. I was just glad the DeBolts weren't obvious abusers and I hoped Virginia didn't get any grand ideas from their example.

Since the DeBolt family encouraged their children to appreciate music and several of the disabled kids played musical instruments, Emelia and I were signed up for piano lessons with a lady from church. We weren't asked if we wanted lessons, it was just done. Virginia explained that she didn't get music lessons as a child because Grandma Quigley couldn't afford them and that we were lucky to learn to play. Virginia had a spinet piano and an impressive Kimball electric organ that Harley gave her on their wedding anniversary. She was proud of her skills as a self-taught pianist and often played the organ and piano at church. Her goal was that Emelia and I would follow her footsteps and be the musical ones in the family. The only problem was I didn't want to learn the piano. I wanted to spend my precious spare time outside, as far away from the house as possible. Our weekly lessons at the piano teacher's house were fun for me. After my turn of being tortured at the keyboard I was able to review her impressive book collection. I was content to sit and read while Emelia took her turn pounding on the black and white keys. I was supposed to be paying attention and benefiting from the teacher's instruction to Emelia but I couldn't muster the energy to fake interest.

After a good long while the piano teacher admitted defeat and confided to Virginia that I not only had no interest in learning piano, I hadn't progressed beyond the beginner piano book. She was convinced I had no natural musical talent. At the same time the teacher delivered the bad news about me, she reported Emelia was making satisfactory progress and showed real promise. She asked to be allowed to drop me and focus her attention solely on Emelia. Overnight I was freed from the daily after school torture of piano practice and resumed my outdoor wanderings. It took Emelia another year to stop trying to please Virginia and the piano teacher. She too was finally released from the seventh ring of hell known as piano practice at our house.

My reprieve from music education didn't end there. Virginia decided that if the piano was beyond my feeble abilities, I might excel at the guitar. Once again, I wasn't given a choice – just another lecture on gratitude and how I should get some. This time it wasn't so bad. My school music teacher taught the guitar class so at least I wasn't the only one lugging a guitar case to school three times a week for lessons. I was supposed to practice every day for 30 minutes. I was allowed to do this in my bedroom with the door shut, which means I didn't do it. Every Friday the music teacher collected practice slips from the students signed by their parents certifying they did the required weekly practicing at home. Since Virginia and Harley weren't paying for private guitar lessons, they didn't know about the practice slips because I didn't tell them. Rather than invite their scrutiny regarding my guitar progress, I came up with my own solution to the practice slip problem. It worked beautifully through the whole school year, including the Christmas and Spring School Music Concerts which Harley and Virginia reluctantly attended. Since I never practiced a lick, I couldn't play anything. There were enough kids in the class the teacher didn't notice I made microscopic progress in my fingering and strumming abilities. Instead of actually learning, I mastered the art of Air Guitar about 20 years before it became popular. I could fake strum and cord positions with the best of them, throwing my body into the groove of the beat without any actual sound coming from my instrument. My enthusiastic guitar acting was convincing enough no one challenged my technique. All went well until after the final school concert of the year. I was in the music room, cleaning out my music cubby. Harley stood at the classroom door, waiting to help me carry my guitar and papers to the car. The teacher, who had never met Harley, made the family connection. "Are you Heather's father?" she said, her hand extended in a warm handshake. "I just want you to know what a wonderful daughter you have. She is a delight in class, doesn't cause any problems and you are a very impressive parent, Mr. Spencer. I have never seen a parent, a father no less, more dedicated to their child's music lessons. Heather has perfect practice slips this year and no student has ever accomplished that before. Thank you for supporting her and signing her slips every week."

She beamed a wide smile at Harley, while he did a slow turn to look at me with a questioning face. "Practice slips? What practice slips?" he asked

. I stood next to him, my head bowed. I was in deep trouble, the kind I had never experienced before in my life. The teacher showed Harley my class folder which held a pile of slips with his signature carefully forged in pencil. I honestly don't remember what happened next. I don't know how we got home or what Harley said to Virginia. I don't know if I got paddled that night or what my Compound Punishment was since I practiced an unthinkable level of deceit. I have no memory of the rest of that story and I am fine with that. All that matters now is I survived and I don't have any noticeable scars.

5. GOD'S FAVORITE FORMS OF TORTURE

As we kids got older, it was harder for them to spank us. We all truly developed buns of steel and didn't cry unless Harley hit us hard enough that he breathed heavy. Virginia couldn't spank us after the first year because she wasn't strong enough to swing with any force. Virginia transitioned into our emotional abuser. I heard Harley tell Virginia he hated to come home from work to find out he had to spank us kids. He said he was already tired and couldn't do a good job of it. Apparently spanking four kids almost nightly is a lot of work. Luckily for him, God gave him a better solution. He announced he had been praying about how to discipline us and said he had a vision. In his dream, he was shown 'The Wall.'

Being on The Wall meant standing flat foot, feet spread as far apart as possible, leaning to the wall, with only the palms of our hands touching the wall. Think of being searched by the police. It doesn't sound that awful, until you have been fully stretched out for about five minutes. After that, our calf and arm muscles began to tire. They moved from merely aching to screaming, then to trembling. The only way to bring relief was to carefully shift our weight from one leg to the other, inching slowly towards the wall, making sure not to make any big movements for fear one of the adults might notice. Virginia contemplated taping down a permanent line on the floor for us to stand on so we would be uniformly stretched out and she could easily see who was cheating. The only problem with this was we kids were varying heights so that idea didn't work.

If we were really in trouble, The Wall was modified so only our fingertips touched the wall. We held that position from the moment our chores were done, with one or two bathroom breaks and maybe a meal break, all day. It was not unusual to be on The Wall for seven or eight hours a day for one or two weeks straight.

This was done in the family room with everyone else watching tv as if nothing was wrong. The family room of course, so the adults could monitor us while they watched their favorite shows. If we were caught trying to lessen the pain by inching our feet closer to the wall, we ran the risk of having more time added on The Wall. This form of torture lasted until I was in seventh grade and Virginia's brother and his family came into town for a rare visit.

I was on The Wall being punished for not including Emelia in my play with the neighborhood kids. Since we hadn't seen any of these relatives in several years, I was interested to see if I would be allowed to stop my punishment when they arrived. I wasn't.

It was obvious my uncle and his family were very uncomfortable visiting my parents with me right next to Virginia's chair, stretched out along the wall. Uncle Don asked if I was doing a stretching exercise and Virginia told him I was being punished. While Virginia was out of the room he sidled up to next to me and whispered, "What did you do to deserve this?"

I told him quietly I didn't include Emelia in a roller-skating contest I was doing with the neighbor kids and would be on The Wall every day after my chores were done for two weeks. It gave me great satisfaction to see his hardened ex-military face react with surprise.

They ended their visit quickly and Uncle Don later called Virginia telling her how upset they were by the harsh treatment they witnessed. Virginia complained to Grandma Quigley that her brother obviously had no experience dealing with difficult children, so who was he to tell her The Wall was too much?

Compared to the terrible abuse Virginia and her brother suffered at the hands of Grandma, this was nothing. Grandma Quigley didn't disagree. She really couldn't, considering how a regular form of entertainment at the Spencer's consisted of everyone, except Rex, gathering in the evening and listening as the adults took turns sharing tales of their youth. Grandma Quigley told us about living as an orphan with a physically abusive Amish family in Lancaster, Pennsylvania.

Next up was Virginia with stories of alcoholic stepfathers who beat her with a cat-o-nine tails until her back and legs bled freely, along with Grandma's Quigley's maternal neglect and abject poverty in the slums of Philadelphia, Pennsylvania. The evening wrapped up with a story or two from Harley about his childhood in Washington State that consisted of harsh beatings and adult level manual labor.

Occasionally we were treated with stories of how Virginia and Harley abused their four biological children, three of whom had died in a horrific house fire years before. Only their oldest son, Marcus survived. The night of the fire he was twelve years-old and babysitting his siblings. He resented being burdened with their care and told them before they went to bed that he wished they were dead. Hours later, at three in the morning, his wish came true. The house erupted into flames from a smoldering chimney fire and Marcus, Harley and Virginia barely escaped with their lives. Marcus suffered a badly broken leg from being thrown out his second story bedroom window by his dad. Harley had burns and smoke inhalation. The house was a total loss, the only surviving photos of their family singed with heat marks.

By the time Rex and I arrived at the Spencers, Marcus had grown up and was married with his own children. Matthew and Emelia were adopted as babies from different families, at least a decade after the fire. There was also another adopted daughter, Shirley, who was married with kids. I didn't understand why the Spencer's adopted her, she was almost eighteen years-old when they took her in. It didn't matter to me since we only saw her and her family at holidays.

From the way Virginia described their three biological children and from the school pictures she showed us, they were cute, smart kids that she beat the crap out of. I felt terrible for them, especially when Virginia talked about bruising their faces with her backhand. Virginia cried and said she missed those children. She wished she had treated them better, like she did us.

I was sad for the terrible abuse Grandma Quigley, Virginia and Harley suffered as children. I agreed that at least we weren't beaten by a cat o'nine tails that drew blood. On the other hand, they sounded like awful parents to their first children. Why did they abuse those innocent children so badly? I didn't dare breathe a word of what I was thinking because I knew my next thought would definitely result in me getting the beating of my life. What I secretly thought was: Thank goodness God rescued those poor children. He took them home to heaven so Virginia and Harley couldn't hurt them anymore.

All the stories of generational abuse solidified in my heart that in my someday family, if I ever got married and had kids, no way was I going to be like they were. I wasn't ever going to spank my kids or treat them like we were. The abuse was ending with me.

The Spencers stories always ended with the same moral lesson: *compared to what we endured and our first children lived with, you kids have nothing to complain about.*

Apparently Uncle Don's comment about seeing us on The Wall made an impression. Shortly thereafter Harley had another dream. He informed us The Wall was no longer an effective punishment tool. From then on, we all received the same punishment as Rex, being sent to our rooms for months at a time.

Finally, after six years of waiting, I got my wish. I was back to how I was treated in the foster home; I was ignored. Yay for me.

6. SAME LIFE, DIFFERENT LOCATION

Within a couple of years of living at the Spencer's, Madeline and McKenzie, Marcus's daughters, came to live with us. Marcus and his wife had divorced and neither of them could raise the girls alone.

Harley and Virginia were given legal charge of the girls, so our nieces became our little sisters. Emelia and I were put in charge of the girls. We potty-trained two year-old McKenzie and played dolls with four year-old Madeline. We shared our bedroom and did everything related to their daily care under the supervision of Virginia and Grandma Quigley. I felt sorry for them. They were very cute and happy and I felt badly they couldn't stay with their mom. I didn't think any more children should be with the Spencers and hoped it would go better for them than it was going for Rex and me.

Harley decided to run for a position on the school board. He filed the paperwork and announced his candidacy without telling Virginia. She found out about it by reading it in the newspaper. She was furious. He had no money, no reputation and the family was going to be the laughing stock of the town. I could see why Harley didn't tell her. To say she was unsupportive puts it mildly.

Harley was working as the facilities superintendent for the school district at the time and was responsible for the maintenance of district buildings. He felt confident about his ideas of streamlining costs and making the schools run more efficiently. He said God wanted him to run for the school board and heavenly help would come from above if we all just stayed faithful.

Not only was his campaign a bust with no money and no support from the community, anyone who knew us kids must have suspected something was wacky. During the campaign allegations were made that Harley had used school owned materials to improve our house, which was technically true. Harley had rescued four wooden cabinets from the dumpster during a school remodeling project and installed them in our kitchen. They were old and scarred up and it took a lot of work on Harley's part to make them look nice, but they were in our kitchen. The scandal was loud enough that not only did he lose the election, but he was fired from his job. Virginia said it was his fault for not withdrawing from the campaign when she told him to. Harley was resolute that bigger blessings were to come because he stayed faithful. Our financial situation derailed quickly.

For several months Harley was on the road, working out of town at temporary construction jobs while trying to find a new job. Virginia cooked at a local 24-hour diner at night. I was surprised. Other than holidays and baking a roast on Sundays, she never cooked. I didn't know she had it in her. Grandma Quigley had always done the daily cooking for us. The best part of Virginia's job was that it was a night shift, when she was normally awake. For the first time since we had been adopted, our evenings were free from adults because Grandma preferred to watch her tv in her own room. Oh Happy Day! We kids didn't bicker about what shows to watch or fight for preferential seating on the couch. We were in heaven to not have Virginia or Harley around in the evening. Even Rex, still banished to his bedroom seemed to relax.

After several months of constant arguing about whose fault it was, Harley's for not quitting the school board campaign or Virginia's for not being supportive of his vision,

Harley got a job in Phoenix, Arizona and we left Oregon. I didn't want to leave what I considered my hometown. Eugene had brought me my first friend and suburban schools where I didn't have to feel on guard all the time. I liked the neighbors who let me eat fruit off their trees and the nearby auto parts store that gave me free STP oil stickers for my bike. I especially liked the family at the end of our street who owned a food truck company and gave us kids their day old donuts for free. At least their pastries weren't moldy or slimy, like the ones we were given at home.

Before we moved we had a garage sale to get rid of a lifetime of crap that Virginia had hoarded. It took days to haul everything out of the attic and out of the overhead storage on the carport. She had enough unpainted ceramics from a pottery phase to fill a store. There were boxes and boxes of clothes, shoes, and every kind of purse imaginable. You know it's bad when people at your garage sale can't believe all this stuff came from one family. In our case, it was one person. Virginia.

When it came time for me to pack my things, it easily fit into four boxes. I carefully printed my name on each box and taped them shut for the moving truck. After we drove three days from the green mountains of Oregon to the beige desert of Arizona, I unpacked my boxes, noticing Claudia's white vinyl purse that I brought from the foster home, the one that had their address and phone number printed on the inside flap, was missing. I asked Grandma Quigley if she thought the mover's might have taken it. Grandma laughed and said, "No, your mom took it out because you don't need it."

I was speechless. Virginia went through my boxes? When did she do that and why? I had so little, why did she take anything of mine? My shock must have shown on my face because Grandma said "You don't need to know about your biological parents. You belong to us now."

I nodded and went back to my room, raging in my heart. Who are they to decide I didn't need my old parents? Then I remembered and frantically checked for the Bedknobs and Broomsticks album. It was still there. Good. I was so glad that

I decided to print my name, my parents name and their address on my album, too. Obviously, Virginia missed that when she pawed through my meager things. What a witch. I hated her. Silently, I mourned my lost ugly vinyl purse for days.

Harley had to sell Virginia's piano and organ to cover the mortgage of our house in Oregon that wasn't selling and the rent in Phoenix. The pretty canopy beds and fancy furniture were sold too. Emelia, Madeline, McKenzie and I all slept in one small bedroom on two plain bunk beds. I was so relieved. I couldn't get hassled anymore about my lack of appreciation for the finer things of life.

Once we moved to Phoenix, Virginia stopped working and she was home all the time. She was always in a terrible mood, complaining that our financial situation was worse than ever. I found that surprising because she moaned about money whether we seemed to have a lot or none. I resented all of it. I wondered why she was able to work in Oregon but not in Arizona. I didn't see any change in her health or any reason she couldn't work. Grandma Quigley was still living with us and could watch over the house while she was gone. Virginia frustrated me because all she did was complain but she didn't do anything to make things better.

Down to one income, Harley not making nearly what he made in Oregon, we qualified for food stamps. Virginia hated being poor and found using food stamps humiliating. She sent us kids to the nearby store, giving us the food stamps so she wouldn't have to use them. I hated doing the grocery shopping. It wasn't the food stamps that bothered me, even though I picked up on the cashier's big sighs and judgmental looks. It was the way Virginia made out the grocery list in handwriting I struggled to decipher and if I guessed wrong and bought the gallon of milk with the yellow label instead of the red label, she would make me turn around in the 100 degree heat and walk back to the store to get the right one. It's friggin' milk, who cares what the label is? Until I learned what Virginia's shopping habits were, it wasn't unusual to make three or more trips to the store to exchange items that didn't suit her tastes. I just wished she would go to the store herself and leave me out of it.

At Christmas, the school nurse from my junior high school came to our house and brought boxes of food. It was more than Virginia could handle. She said they were in such desperate straits because of us kids.

More than once I had to bite my tongue to stop myself from retorting, "Please tell us why you ever adopted kids. It's obvious you don't like us."

Instead we all stood silently, agreeing in the collective stillness that her lot in life was hard. What other option did we have? I hated being a child, unable to point out the obvious power she had as an adult to get a job and do something. I couldn't understand why she was content to do nothing but complain. It was exhausting to hear every day how my mere existence on the planet was a burden to her.

All of the kids in the family were quickly made targets in our respective schools. We were white country bumpkins who previously attended small suburban schools. There were no African Americans, Hispanics or any other race other than white in our world. None of us had ever heard of gangs or possessed the skills needed to survive in our new tough, inner city schools that had security guards and locked gates. We were all sitting ducks. For the first time, I had a taste of what Rex had gone through in school for years. All of us struggled to find a circle of friends. I missed my friend Leslie like crazy. For Rex it was all status quo.

The situation didn't cause us kids to grow closer to each other. Instead, it magnified the weaknesses in the family. There was no talk of being poor, white and defenseless. We all just sucked it up and pretended everything was fine. No one ever told Virginia how difficult it was surviving in a school of over a thousand students. There was no point. Compared to her suffering, past and present, we had nothing to complain about.

I don't know when Rex quit trying, I just know he did. He stopped talking to Virginia, Harley and Grandma Quigley. He didn't talk to any of us kids, either. I quit, too. I quit hoping things would get better. I realized with the Spencers, every time I thought things had hit rock bottom and surely they would be forced to change, that didn't happen. Instead things went from bad to worse and then even worse than that. There was no end in sight and Rex and I were trapped forever. We both gave up the dream of having parents who loved us. The Spencers broke whatever spirit we had and it was gone for good.

By then it had been so long since Rex had eaten dinner with the family, I had forgotten it was even a possibility. Virginia didn't check to see if he did his chores and over time, he wasn't assigned any. Rex was never going to eat dinner ever again.

At school Rex hung around the cafeteria asking for food. The kitchen workers sometimes took pity on him and gave him leftovers at the end of the lunch periods. Since Rex and I didn't have the same lunch hour, I didn't realize what he was doing until one of the kitchen supervisors told me to tell Rex to quit hanging around the school kitchen. When I snuck into Rex's bedroom to relay the message, embarrassed beyond belief at the thought of him begging for food, he said nothing. He only shrugged his shoulders and went back to reading his smuggled science fiction book.

Rex still wet the bed every night and the boys' bedroom took on the smell of a urinal. I don't know how Matthew stood it, but he didn't complain. I guessed being cured of autism helped him handle intolerable situations. Rex slept on his yellow pee-stained plastic covered mattress on the floor.

Since Rex didn't stop wetting the bed and still occasionally wet himself during the day, Virginia decided he didn't deserve new clothes until he took pride in the clothes he already had. He wore pants that were painfully short, his ankles and dingy white socks filling in the empty space between his pants and the top of his worn out tennis shoes. His wrists cleared his shirt sleeves by several inches and his too small shirts hugged his thin ribcage. As Matthew got new clothes he gave his old clothes to Rex, so at least once a year at back to school time Rex got some clothes that fit better for a while. He was totally dependent on Matthew's growing spurts. By the time Matthew was done with his tennis shoes and jeans, there wasn't much to pass on.

Another change after our arrival in Phoenix was that Matthew, Rex, Emelia and I were expected to buy our own clothes, shoes, shampoo, toothpaste, soap, toilet paper, sanitary supplies, and anything else we needed that Virginia didn't want to buy for us.

Grandma Quigley bought toiletries for Madeline and McKenzie with her Social Security check and she kept their supplies in her room. If they needed to use the restroom, they would stop at Grandma's room to pick up a roll of tissue then return it to her for safe keeping. Other than basic food, shelter and utilities, if we needed something we had to get it for ourselves. Once I got my first job working full-time during the summer at a government-subsidized job for teenagers, I figured out how to budget my money to cover the necessities. Before I could formally work, I babysat and while in other people's homes I stole feminine supplies, soap and whatever else I needed that I could fit in my purse and pockets.

When I was a freshman in high school, I needed a new winter coat. Living in Phoenix, where the temperature soars to 115 degrees in the summer it might seem silly to need a coat but during the winter months the overnight temperatures dip below freezing. I didn't dare ask Virginia for a coat. I knew better. I discovered the Lost and Found box at school. In the main office was a box of clothes, shoes and other things that students had left behind. I spied a nice brown corduroy jacket that looked like it was in good shape. I pretended the coat was mine and that I was glad to have it back. The secretary behind the desk didn't blink an eye at my behavior and let me rummage through the box to check if any of my other things were in there. As I was fake looking, I decided it was too risky to take a pair of shoes or other clothes. The chances of the real owners recognizing their stuff was too great. I settled for just the coat and left the office before anyone could question me. The coat was way too big and was obviously for a boy, but I didn't care. I was just so glad to be warm. A few of my friends commented on my new coat but I pretended I had it for a long time and they just hadn't noticed. I lived with low-grade anxiety the rest of winter, fearful the real owner of the coat would see it and accuse me of stealing it, but thankfully no one did. After spring came I relaxed, assuming since the coat was large that it must belong to a senior boy who would be graduating soon. I wore the coat until I was a senior and could afford to buy a new coat for $15 on clearance at the mall. I don't know what Rex wore or if he even had a coat. We moved every year in Phoenix, always staying in the same area so we kids could continue in the same school, changing houses when our leases were up. Virginia said it was too expensive for us kids to use the clothes dryer. We had good backs and were perfectly able to hang our laundry, while the adults used the dryer. It wasn't a big deal to us kids, we had been hanging our clothes for a while. In one rental house someone stole my clothes off the backyard clothes line. When my clothes disappeared, I panicked. All my clothes, other than what I was wearing, were on that line and now they were gone. I had only the pants and shirt I was wearing and a few pairs of socks, a stray pair of panties and a bra. Virginia said it was my fault for not watching the clothes line better. Who steals clothes off a clothes line? I had never heard of such a thing but was not surprised when it was turned into being my fault.

I had no babysitting money at the time, so I had no choice but to wear the same clothes to school every day, washing them out in the bathroom sink and hanging them in my bedroom to dry overnight. I had no answer for the teasing I took at school. I was humiliated and burning with hatred for Virginia, Harley and Grandma Quigley. I also had a tiny insight into what Rex had been suffering all his life.

That weekend the heavens smiled down on me. While walking in the neighborhood I saw one of my shirts in the middle of a front lawn. I grabbed it, furtively looking around for more. I saw my pants under bushes, my socks left in driveways, my dresses hanging from trees, all my clothes scattered over a full block. I joyfully gathered my clothes like I was picking fruit from a bounteous garden. I was so grateful to have my thrift store clothes back. A few days later Emelia told me our pot-smoking, teenage neighbor laughingly confessed to her that he had taken my clothes and scattered them for fun. I thanked her for telling me and never left my clothes out to dry in the backyard again. I didn't tell Virginia that I found my clothes. I doubt she even noticed. I didn't feel too bad when a month later our lease was up and we moved on, leaving the landlord with the biological results of Emelia's escaped pet mice who had multiplied in shocking numbers. I shook a baby mouse out of the dining room hutch as we picked it up to carry it to the moving truck. I telepathically directed the mouse to run to our next door neighbor's house and bite the teenager who took my clothes.

Getting toiletries was a problem for Rex. Because he was always grounded to his room, he couldn't get a job or even mow lawns for neighbors like Matthew did. Occasionally there were squabbles in the bathroom over Rex stealing someone else's toilet paper or soap. He began a habit of using a kitchen sponge to wipe himself clean after using the toilet, then rinsing it out in the sink. When I realized that is what his sponge was for, I made a point of not touching it, but I didn't say anything to him about it. I didn't have a better solution to his problem and was a bit surprised he thought of using the sponge. It wouldn't have occurred to me as a possibility. I never thought to ask how he took care of himself, I was too consumed trying to meet my own needs.

When Emelia started her menstrual cycle, she went to Virginia and asked for supplies. Virginia made a huge deal out of it in front of the rest of the family, asking exactly what Emelia needed and how much it was going to cost. Virginia launched into a story about how when she was a girl they were too poor for feminine products and how she wasn't even told about menstrual cycles by Grandma Quigley. A nun at Virginia's Catholic school had to explain it to her and the nun showed her how to fold newspaper to make a pad to absorb the blood. After the story was over Emelia was confused, hoping Virginia wasn't telling her to use folded newspaper as sanitary napkins. Emelia asked, "Can we go to the store and get napkins?"

Virginia huffed and told Harley to take Emelia to the store to get what she needed. As they left the house Virginia's parting shot was, "And don't think I'm gonna do this every month."

Emelia's face burned with shame. I was outraged. What kind of way was that to treat a girl who got her first period? It wasn't like it wasn't still happening to her. She had such heavy periods that later that same year, Virginia had a hysterectomy. While she was in the hospital for her surgery, I prayed she would die and we would be set free. I felt guilty for praying that, but I was working on being honest about my feelings to God. My Sunday school teacher said that Heavenly Father didn't listen to repetitive, worn out prayers. When we prayed to Him, we needed to be completely honest and tell Him everything; the good, the bad, everything and that He would understand and comfort us. I figured I didn't have much to lose by telling God the truth. When Virginia hobbled in the front door, discharged from the hospital, I was a tad bit disappointed Heavenly Father didn't help me out.

After witnessing the humiliation Emelia went through, when my period came a year later I didn't breathe a word to anyone. I went to the public library and got a book about puberty and learned all I needed to know and handled it myself. That was the beginning of my figuring out that anything I needed to learn in life was in a book.

Living with the Spencers was my experience of what it must have been like living under Nazi rule during World War II. Harley and Virginia instructed us to pay attention to what each other was doing and then report any misdeed back to the adults. They reasoned if they didn't love us, they wouldn't bother disciplining us. I thought their way of showing love was crap, but wasn't 100% sure I disagreed until I saw it in action. When we gave really good information about each other, we were rewarded with high praise and treats. I stopped giving reports after the first time I was turned in by Emelia for some minor infraction and was punished. I learned to not say anything to anyone in the house beyond discussing the weather. Even the most innocent comment could be twisted and used against me. When I ran into any of my siblings at school or in public places, I ignored them. Anything else was too risky. No way was I going to introduce my friends to my siblings. It was every man for himself. Virginia complained I was ungrateful and secretive because I didn't talk about school or my friends, not even with Emelia, with whom I shared a bedroom.

I survived the Spencers by finding teachers at school and leaders at church whom I confided. I tested the waters with adults by telling a small story of some recent trouble I had been in at home and what my punishment had been. If they seemed surprised or asked any follow up questions, I cautiously gave more details. If they didn't react or ask any more questions, I knew they couldn't be trusted. In eighth grade, I found an adult I could trust and who ended up carrying me until I turned eighteen.

Joe Gross was the school librarian at my junior high school. He was a humorous, friendly man who decorated his library with kooky stuff. My friend Teresa, a star athlete at school, introduced me to him. I picked her as my best friend after I saw her tell a group of menacing girls to get the hell away from another girl they were harassing. The mean girls wordlessly obeyed Teresa and I knew right then she was going to save me, too. I complimented her basketball skills and that was the beginning of having a bodyguard. I was intrigued the first day we went to the library instead of hanging out on the basketball courts during lunch recess. I hadn't pegged Teresa as much of a reader.

I loved to read. As a young child in the foster home, a green Bookmobile came to our neighborhood from the local library. That worked for me because Dorothy never took us anywhere and there was no chance she was going to take us foster kids to the library. Because of the bookmobile I was able to get books by myself without needing adult permission. My real mother, Claudia was also a rabid reader, her house was always stacked with books on every flat surface.

When Teresa took me to the school library for the first time, I was disappointed. It was a windowless room, not very big and the selection seemed limited. It reminded me of a cave. I wandered around the shelves, checking for my favorite titles.

Teresa stopped at Mr. Gross's desk and it didn't take long for it to become obvious why she came. Teresa told Mr. Gross about a recent incident at home. He listened to her story, all the while checking in a stack of books that was permanently planted next to his chair. Occasionally he would interrupt her long enough to tell someone to quit leaning back in their chair or quit fooling around in his library. I liked him immediately. His dark hair, long nose and full beard made perfect sense when he told me he was Jewish. I had vague memories of attending Jewish Sabbath Services while in the foster home. I liked the music during the children's class and that the Jewish children's program was more fun than the Catholic Mass I attended with the foster kids.

Teresa and a handful of other kids hung out with Mr. Gross before school, joking and occasionally talking about serious topics. Since I kept my longstanding practice of getting up early and leaving for school as soon as possible, it wasn't hard to join the early morning group in the library. It also had the extra bonus of limiting any bullying, since mean kids didn't go to the library. It didn't seem to bother Mr. Gross that none of the kids in the group checked out books. He appeared to enjoy their company. I thought the idea of a teacher who actually talked to kids was quite novel. Over the course of the school year Mr. Gross became my friend and mentor.

I told him I was seriously thinking of running away but couldn't figure out how to do it without ending up living on the streets. I hadn't forgotten the lessons I learned from my first escape attempt at six years-old. He told me it wasn't a good idea and probably the best thing to do would be to just hang in there until I was eighteen. After all, I had made it this far. I thought about it and realized he was right. Rex and I would just have to make it a few more years. As soon as I turned eighteen, we were going to disappear and the Spencers would never see us again. The thought cheered me up immensely. The sentence "I've made it this far," became my mantra.

Mr. Gross made me promise not to quit school and to make graduating high school my goal. He pointed out that the only way to get a good job was to have a diploma. Otherwise, I would be doomed to minimum wage jobs forever. Until he suggested it, I hadn't thought of high school graduation as something to make as a goal. I was just floating along, trying to deal with the short term. I was making decent enough grades but I wasn't thrilled about learning. I liked school because it got me away from home. I would have liked anything that got me away from the Spencers.

With Mr. Gross's encouragement, I started dreaming of a future where Rex and I lived in our own place, taking care of ourselves. We had already survived six years of adoptive hell with five more to go. We were more than halfway there.

Over time I shared most of my life with Mr. Gross, except what was going on at home with Rex. I knew in my heart that Mr. Gross would report it to the authorities if he knew how bad it was. I thought that if the police got involved it would only make it worse. I remembered what happened the last time the police came to the Spencers house. I didn't know what could happen, I just knew it wouldn't be good. It was too big of a risk, better to just lay low and wait it out. Besides, Rex went to school every day. There were plenty of adults with eyes to see if they wanted to.

I also thought Mr. Gross wouldn't like me anymore

if he knew I wasn't protecting Rex from Virginia and Harley. I was afraid to lose his good opinion of me. I had to keep my secret to myself. When my period arrived in the eighth grade, every month I experienced severe pain with my cycle. Mr. Gross recommended I tell my parents and get it checked out. I laughed and told him, "No thanks. It's not worth it. I'm sure it will get better." What I didn't say was that I hadn't been to a doctor or dentist since I left the foster home. None of us kids ever went for checkups. If we were sick, Virginia had a big bottle of antibiotics that she bought from a veterinary store on top of the refrigerator and we took those until we felt better. If we were sick enough to get Virginia's attention, she gave us a shot in our butt of liquid antibiotics she bought at the same veterinary store. Thankfully, my pain did go away on its own within six months and I didn't have any problems after that. I was relieved I didn't have to trust my health to the Spencers. Luckily, the rest of us hardly ever got sick and when we did, we kept it to ourselves. The less we asked of them, the better.

In junior high Emelia flunked the spine screen at school and was referred for treatment of scoliosis. Virginia took her to a doctor who explained she needed to wear a body brace to help straighten her spine but Emelia refused because the ugly brace would have killed her social life. Since she didn't want to wear a brace, she was given exercises to do to strengthen her back. She did them once in a while, but not enough to help. That was the end of doctor's treatments for her spine. When Emelia complained about her back hurting, Virginia reminded her it was her own fault.

The one rare time that we asked something of Virginia and we actually got it without justifying a need, I was mystified as to how it happened. Emelia decided she wanted a pet rabbit. She told me she was going to ask Harley if she could have one. I didn't think she had a chance in hell of that happening, considering we already had a bunch of neglected, wild dogs in the back yard that we paid no attention to other than to feed and water them. I tried to play with them, but they were so dirty and tick-covered, it was sad to be around them. They were Virginia's dogs, not ours, so I didn't give them much thought.

When Emelia said Harley thought it was a great idea to get rabbits, I couldn't believe it. Really? We could have pets of our very own? This was a new development. Until then, Virginia brought home dogs and cats without discussing it and we kids would be responsible for feeding and watering them.

Emelia and I went with Harley to pick out our new pet rabbits. I picked a jet black rabbit, Emelia got a multi-colored one. We bought cages, food and water bottles. The cages were placed in the back yard and Emelia and I became rabbit owners. I named mine after the Cat Stevens song, "Moonshadow." I sang, "I'm being followed by a moonshadow, moonshadow, moonshadow" as I petted the rabbit and watched it eat the green rabbit pellet food. It was blazing hot in the Phoenix heat so I draped wet towels over Moonshadow's cage to help him stay cool. After six months of watching my pet rabbit grow to fill its cage, I came home from school one day to see something odd in the refrigerator. Soaking in salted water in the large Tupperware bowl we used for salads was raw meat. It looked like scrawny chicken meat without the skin. I had never seen anything like that before and wondered what someone was going to do with it. Emelia came up behind me, standing in front of the open fridge and whispered it was our rabbits. "What?" I asked, panic in my chest. "Our rabbits? What happened? Who did that?"

I thought there must have been an accident. Emelia shrugged and walked away. I went into the family room, where Virginia was sitting in her recliner, watching tv. "Is that my rabbit in the fridge?" I asked.

Virginia replied, not taking her eyes off the tv, "Of course. Your father butchered them this morning. You didn't think we would waste money feeding animals for nothing, did you? We are eating them for dinner tonight."

My mind reeled. They slaughtered my Moonshadow. I remembered my skepticism when Emelia asked for rabbits. Now I knew why they agreed to it with no complaints. They were planning on this from the beginning. Harley whistled in the kitchen as he battered and fried the rabbits for dinner. I refused to eat, horrified they would think I could eat my pet. They gave my dinner to Rex, who was happy to get anything.

7. I GOT HEAVEN COVERED

During our years in foster care, all us kids went to church at whichever denomination was willing to offer door-to-door service. I have distinct memories of the Catholic, Evangelical and Jewish children's classes. Our religious education was reserved for Sunday morning only, with no adult participation. It was a time for Dorothy to get a break from us.

On our weekends with Ralph and Claudia, my brother and I attended services at the Jehovah Witness Hall that was across the street from their house. Claudia was a devoted Witness and her fervent beliefs sometimes created problems for us at the foster home. Claudia didn't want Ezra and me to participate in Halloween trick-or-treating, which was against the Jehovah Witness's religious tenants. She asked Dorothy to make sure the other kids shared their candy with us, which of course, they didn't want to do. Claudia also didn't want us involved in any other festivities, but Dorothy found it too difficult to deny us the treats and parties she gave the other children on holidays. We received Easter Baskets and Christmas presents from Dorothy and our birthdays were celebrated in the foster home.

After we moved to the Spencer's house we were introduced to their religious faith. They were members of The Church of Jesus Christ of Latter-day Saints, or Mormons as they are commonly referred to. Rex was nine years-old when we were adopted, which meant he was old enough to be baptized into the church right away.

We both took lessons with missionaries who explained the history of the church and its beliefs. Rex was eager to talk to the missionaries and asked very detailed questions, absorbing the theology like a sponge. I wasn't so interested. I just enjoyed goofing around with the 19 year-old missionaries after our lessons. They were a lot of fun and didn't mind a seven year-old who wanted to pretend arm wrestle with them.

Rex enjoyed Primary, the children's Sunday school program. He liked singing and participating in the games and storytelling. I wasn't all that fond of church. Compared to other churches we went to in foster care, this one was much longer and required a lot more sitting and paying attention. They sang way more and expected me to sing too. And most annoying, they didn't feed us cookies during classes. The Catholic and Jewish children's programs were way better.

By the time I turned eight years-old, which is considered the age of accountability and typically when baptism takes place, I had made friends with the kids my age at church and it was ok. Besides, what choice did I have? I didn't want to be a Jehovah's Witness like Ralph and Claudia. I liked birthdays, the Fourth of July and Christmas and Easter candy. I didn't have any strong feelings about any church, even though I had been to plenty. Just like everything else, my religion was decided by the adults. My God was now a Mormon God. I assumed the Jewish, Catholic, Evangelical and Jehovah's Witness Gods would understand.

The Spencers presented themselves as being a wonderful, loving family that took in unfortunate children. At church they held leadership positions and put up a good front as being super parents doing Christian work with us kids. Nothing was worse than having to sing hymns like "Love at Home" while I was being pinched by Virginia for not sitting up straight in the pew. But what could I do? Since the Spencers were smart enough to move their abuse away from belts and bruises, I couldn't prove anything.

As we became teenagers, the physical disparity between Rex being unkempt and painfully skinny and the rest of us kids who were well fed and clean, was quite obvious. Every time someone questioned Rex's condition, Virginia had a story of what a difficult child he was and how he preferred to look unkempt rather than take care of himself. Every concern about Rex was explained away as being a residual problem from our terrible years in foster care. We were so badly abused there that the Spencers were doing everything they could and it still wasn't enough.

For Rex, even church wasn't a safe haven. He tried to play with the young children but was shooed away by adults. The kids his own age teased him and called him "weirdo." He constantly missed social cues and would say inappropriate things. Rex was an eight year-old boy trapped in a teenager's body. Most of the time I ignored his behavior or would get mad at him for bringing trouble onto himself. I tried very hard to fit in with our peers and was frustrated when Rex couldn't follow the program. My brother embarrassed me and I didn't want anyone to think I was like him. I wanted to have friends and be invited to parties and sleepovers and someday, maybe even have a boy who liked me enough to kiss me. That wasn't going to happen with Rex hanging around, making people feel uncomfortable.

Before the 1980's churches weren't aggressive in reporting perceived neglect cases. Unless there were broken bones or marks, the burden of proof kept situations like ours in the background. As society's attitudes of parental authority have changed so has the response from most churches. I like to think the kind of abuse Rex suffered then would not be tolerated by any religious community now and would have been reported to local authorities.

Sometimes church accidentally contributed to Rex's suffering. One night in our teens we attended a 'Fireside' at the home of a church member. Firesides are evening meetings held on Sundays to give the young people an opportunity to discuss gospel topics relevant to them. The boys and girls from our congregation ages 14-18 years-old were invited and all the adult leaders of the Young Men and Young Women's organization attended. Usually they are very casual meetings with a healthy dose of covert flirting between the kids.

The guest speaker was a waiter at the local ice cream shop who happened to be a member of our church and had just moved to town as an aspiring comedian. Everyone was looking forward to an evening of professional entertainment. The house was packed. Rex sat down on the floor right in front of the comedian, who was a good-looking guy in his mid-twenties.

The speaker began by introducing himself, telling us the places he had performed, one of which was a Playboy Club in Las Vegas. It was obvious the church leaders didn't know much about this comedian. As he began his "shtick" it consisted mainly of ridiculing the audience. First everyone in the room was fair game, and the teasing hit the popular kids too. But when the comedian saw how everyone roared with laughter when he commented on Rex, he focused on Rex. He berated Rex's clothes, his greasy hair, his crooked smile and the way he nervously blinked, mimicking perfectly Rex's mannerisms.

At first Rex laughed along, trying to get the joke. When it didn't stop his face turned red and he balled up his fists with anger. That just gave the comedian more ammunition. I was ashamed and wished the adults would stop the comedian from making fun of Rex, but no one did. Finally Rex had enough of the ridicule and stormed out of the room. The comedian called out, "Hey, buddy, don't be a spoiled sport, I was only kidding."

That was one of the rare times I did the right thing. I got up and followed Rex out. The adult leaders caught us outside in the driveway and tried to get us to come back inside. Rex had tears streaming down his face. I felt terrible for laughing with the group at my brother's expense. The evening broke up shortly after that. I don't recall anyone apologizing to Rex, I'm sure they did, not that it mattered. Even at church he wasn't safe from the world's cruelties. No adult leaders took him under their wing. All they did was ask the kids to be nice to Rex, but it didn't work. Nothing else was done. The best Rex could hope for at church was to be ignored, just like at home.

8. REJECTION, AGAIN

Rex did have excellent taste in women. In his sophomore year, he developed a crush on a beautiful cheerleader. She had long brown hair, brown eyes and a golden complexion. I could see why Rex liked her, everyone did. At first, his attempts to talk to her were small and she was nice to him. She smiled and said, "Thanks," when he complimented her clothes or hair. He began following her from class to class trying to make conversation. She was polite and friendly, but it was obvious she was way out of his league.

It got much harder for her when Rex approached while she was with her friends, the popular kids. Rex ignored everyone's rude comments and butted into the circle, demanding her attention. It wasn't long before the cheerleader's football-playing boyfriend threatened to flatten Rex if he didn't back off and leave his girlfriend alone.

One day the cheerleader found me at my locker and said, "I need to you to tell your brother to leave me alone. I tried being nice to him but it didn't work and now my boyfriend is really mad. Tell him I don't like him and he needs to stop. Oh, and tell him to quit following me home. It's creepy."

I was speechless. First, I had no idea one of the most popular girls in school even knew who I was, and second, I wasn't aware of the depth of Rex's crush on her. I noticed him hanging around on the edges of her group but I didn't know they talked at all. My rule of not talking to my brothers and sisters in public included Rex. I knew more about my classmates than I did my own siblings.

That afternoon I told Rex what she had said, editing it so it wouldn't sound so harsh. After I was done relaying the message, Rex shrugged his shoulders and said, "Oh, I'm not afraid of her boyfriend."

I told Rex he should be. Her boyfriend was a known bully and had a short fuse.

The romance stopped shortly thereafter when the cheerleader, in front of her boyfriend and other friends, loudly told Rex to "leave me alone and keep your stinky distance because you smell like shit."

I witnessed that exchange and stepped in to pull Rex away. Rex came quietly, without argument and I didn't say anything. Sometimes there just isn't anything that can be said.

When Rex was sixteen years-old, Harley and Virginia decided they were done. Beating him, humiliating him, isolating him and starving him didn't work. Rex just was too stubborn and lazy, always daydreaming and in his own little world. His bowel problems continued to plague him and occasionally he still had accidents.

The Spencers tried the 'dirty underwear around the neck treatment' just as our foster father Wayne did, only they upped the humiliation by telling Rex he had to wear it to school, too. Thankfully he took off the feces-filled underpants and hid it in the shrub in our front yard. He put it back on before entering the house after school. Rex acted like it was no big deal.

He completely disconnected and had no emotional response to anything Harley and Virginia heaped on him. One Saturday afternoon their frustration with Rex became too much and they called him out of his bedroom. Virginia announced that since he wasn't willing to do chores properly and did nothing to contribute, he was no longer part of the family. She told him to get his stuff together because he wasn't spending another night in their home.

I listened from my bedroom doorway, amazed. This took their abuse to a whole new level. They were putting Rex out like the trash that was hauled to the front curb. I stayed put, with my door closed except for a slight crack I could see and hear from. After a few minutes Virginia called out to Rex and asked if he was done packing.

His body appeared in the hallway, his back to me. He had a medium-sized light blue camping backpack, the kind Boy Scouts use. I think it was an old backpack Matthew used as a scout. He walked into the living room where Harley and Virginia were waiting. Harley said, "We love you and when you are willing to change you can come back."

Rex said nothing.

Harley opened the front door and Rex stepped out onto the front stoop. Harley shut the door behind him. They went back into the family room and turned the tv on. Mission Accomplished. The rest of us kids pretended nothing happened. To say something would only put their attention on us. Best to stay invisible.

Rex didn't leave the way they thought he would. He had no money, no food, no friends, no car and no connections at school or church. We lived in the suburbs of Phoenix in the middle of miles of identical houses broken only by gas stations, fast food joints and strip malls. He was thirty miles from the nearest homeless shelter. There was nowhere for him to go. Rex snuck back to the house at night and slept on the back patio.

After three nights of Rex sleeping out back, curled up with the pack of matted, tick and flea infested poodles that were the result of Virginia's abandoned attempt at dog breeding, she worried the neighbors would notice and call the police. Harley and Virginia told Rex he had a choice. They would either drive him to skid row in downtown Phoenix or they would buy him a bus ticket back to Oregon. Either way, he was never to return. Rex chose Oregon.

I cringe now, realizing during the three days Rex lived in homeless limbo I never even thought of talking to him. I had nothing to say, no solution to offer. I was furious at what Harley and Virginia did but was I really shocked? No. Had they crossed a new line of abuse in regards to Rex? No. It was completely fathomable and in my heart I was not surprised. And yet I did nothing. My 6 year-old self would have protested loudly, packing her bags and joining her brother instantly, knowing we were a team that could not be broken. But my teenage self was worn down and numb. I didn't have any fight left, just a survival instinct to protect myself. I let my brother go without a sound and my soul barely registered his absence.

9. A NEW BEGINNING

Ralph and Claudia had no idea what happened to us when we disappeared from their lives in Oregon, but the Spencers had information about them. Virginia called directory assistance in Portland and got their phone number. Ralph and Claudia kept their phone number and stayed in the same house so we would be able to find them. Being valiant Jehovah Witnesses, they prayed to God for our safe return. "Jehovah will provide" was their daily prayer.

Once again listening from my bedroom door, overhearing Virginia speak to Claudia, I was relieved. I remembered being anxious around Ralph and Claudia on our weekend visits as a child, not sure what to expect, but after a few hours of play, I would relax and the time with them was peaceful. I felt Rex would be safe with them.

I watched emotionless from my bedroom window while Harley loaded Rex, his tattered coat and backpack into the car to be driven to the bus station. Unlike Rex, I had developed a strong network of friends and connections who could help if it got too bad. I also knew I couldn't help protect either of us if things went wrong in Oregon.

Claudia was thrilled to get the phone call saying Rex was coming, but it created a problem for them. Upon discussing it with others, they decided Rex would have to live with Lennis, Claudia's mother, instead of with Ralph and Claudia. They feared if the state of Oregon found out Rex was back living with them, they would take him away again.

Only once, a few weeks after Rex left, did Virginia mention a phone call from Oregon. Lennis complained Rex was bossing them around, wouldn't shower and all he did was eat. That confirmed everything the Spencers believed. Rex was lazy and stubborn. I thought, "At least he's getting food."

I wish I could say we kept in touch, but we didn't. It was too risky to ask for his address to write. Virginia had a rule that no one was allowed to receive mail without her seeing it first. I knew she would open and throw away any letter from Rex. If I called Information to get his phone number in Portland the extra charge would show up on the bill. It was best to dissolve into the woodwork and wait until I was eighteen and on my own.

Rex wasn't mentioned in the Spencer's house again. We didn't have family pictures on the walls after the first year we were adopted, so it was as if he never existed. At church and school the story was Rex went to live with extended family in Oregon. No one questioned it. He could have died and no one would have batted an eye.

After Rex left, Emelia became the next target of Virginia and Harley's wrath. She was criticized for the clothes she wore, how much makeup she put on and the attention she received from boys. As a last ditch effort to get Emelia away from boys, Virginia dug deep into her pockets and paid for Emelia to take modeling classes at a local agency. Emelia liked it, but all the other girls were from rich families who bought them nice clothes. She was ostracized for not having good enough outfits to wear on the catwalk and soon dropped out. Although I was amazed Virginia paid for the modeling classes, I was really mad at her for not understanding Emelia needed decent clothes to succeed. What a set up for failure.

When the Spencers discovered Emelia was pregnant by her high school boyfriend, Virginia and Grandma Quigley were very upset. Grandma looked up at me from her perch on the couch and said, "I always thought you would be the one who got knocked up. Never Emelia."

Virginia nodded in agreement.

I was insulted, thinking, "Since when have I ever done anything to give you that idea?"

Realizing they both had the expectation I would end up a teenage mother I was determined to prove them wrong. It wasn't hard to do. I had terrible acne, a gigantic gap between my front teeth and I took no serious interest in my appearance.

Harley had dental insurance to cover a portion of the orthodontics I needed, but neither Harley or Virginia were interested in going into debt so I could have straight teeth. That was left to me to figure out when I was a grown up.

I didn't have the money to dress fashionably or to get my hair cut (friends and church members cut my hair) so I didn't have boys interested in me. Emelia was the family beauty, not me.

The one good thing about the modeling classes is they taught Emelia how to wear make-up properly. I bet Emelia looked very pretty on her wedding day at the courthouse. I don't know for sure, no one from our family went to the ceremony.

Around the same time as Emelia's departure with her new husband, Madeline and McKenzie's dad came back into our lives. Marcus had remarried and wanted his daughters back. They had lived with us for all of their childhoods. I was worried. I never cared for Marcus; he had a mean streak just like Virginia and Harley. Having been abused just as badly as his siblings that died in the tragic house fire, I didn't trust Marcus and stayed away from him. I was worried about the girls living with him, but I had no power to stop it.

Within a two year span, Rex was gone, Emelia was married with a baby and Madeline and McKenzie were with their dad and new stepmother. Matthew and I were the only ones left at home with Grandma Quigley and Harley and Virginia. Matthew was jokingly referred to as 'the help' because he did all the yard work and whatever chores were asked of him and he did them very well. He had no friends, no regular job or social life of his own and existed at home to serve. His autism appeared to protect him. He never showed any emotional reaction to anything and seemed perfectly fine. I don't know how he did it.

I learned to do my chores of cooking and cleaning the kitchen without complaint. I did them well enough not to get punished for slothfulness. My biggest sin and what kept me continually grounded most of high school was my attitude. It wasn't enough for me to be obedient, hardworking and quiet. I had to smile and respond to every request with cheerfulness. Screw them. I didn't care if I was grounded or not. I didn't have a social life outside of school anyway. Being grounded to my room at night and on the weekends meant they forgot about me and left me alone so I could disappear into books. Thank God for books. I had a small insight into why my biological mother, Claudia read all the time. I was doing the same thing and I imagined Rex was too. We all three used books as a way to escape things we could not change.

Virginia had an amazing ability to lecture. If I did something she didn't like I would be subjected to a lecture of one to two hours, during which I was forced to stand in front of her recliner. If I did not have my eyes directly on her the whole time, as a show of respect, my grounding to my room would lengthen for several more months over the original offense. I rarely did anything wrong anymore, I just couldn't fake a happy smile enough to suit Virginia and Harley. In a million years I would have never talked back or directly challenged them. That would have been a deadly offense.

As for being grounded to my room for months at a time, I didn't care. Only a fool would spend time in the family room where Virginia watched tv all day and night. Being there opened me to being her servant, available to her beck and call.

One evening Virginia had me running, getting fresh ice for her ever-present Pepsi glass, finding the tv remote that slipped down the inside of her recliner and was under her chair, handing her magazines just out of her reach, bringing her the telephone. It was endless duty and had to be accomplished with a cheerful smile lest I open myself for punishment for having a negative attitude.

This night Virginia was particularly prickly and I was longing for a way to exit the room without causing a problem for myself. After a few hours of silent suffering while cursing myself for being stupid enough to get sucked into the family room by a tv program and now paying a high price for that moment of entertainment, I had my opportunity to make a break for freedom.

Virginia leaned back in her recliner and stretched, yawning loudly. Then she swung her massive body forward and propelled herself to her feet. She sighed as she shuffled past me, saying, "Boy, I sure wish you could go to bathroom for me. Then I wouldn't have to get up at all."

She laughed at her joke as she glanced at me. The thought of Virginia being too lazy to go to the bathroom enraged me but I kept my head down, pretending not to hear. As soon as she was in her bathroom, I made my escape and scooted quickly to my room. Hoping for an end to being the evening's maid, I was ready to relax in peace and quiet. The motto in our house was "Children should be seen and not heard." I also understood, "Out of sight, out of mind." The less interaction with them, the better.

The only escape any of us had from serving time in our bedrooms was attending church services. The Wednesday night youth group activities at church were a lifeline I clung to. I used the hall telephone to call friends. None of my friends ever called our house because all calls were required to be taken in Virginia's presence so she could listen to them. I was able to do the typical teenage checking in with my friends on Wednesday evenings from 6:30 p.m. to 8:30 p.m. during church activities as long as I slipped in and out of services and didn't keep any conversation very long.

When I was a junior in high school I had my first real boyfriend. I don't count my three month whirl-wind romance in 8th grade because that was with John, the bishop's son from church. We kept our fling limited to school hours during the week. At church we pretended to not know each other. We passed notes back and forth at school every day and I allowed him to hold my hand. I wouldn't let him kiss me, but I have to give him credit for trying. Our love ended when I tried to be romantic and wrote John a letter declaring my deep affection for him and I mailed it to his house. Who would have thought his dad had the same exact first and last name? The following Sunday at church John's mom showed Virginia my letter. Lesson learned: Never, ever name a child after a parent. It causes nothing but pain and embarrassment.

I had crushes on lots of boys my freshman and sophomore years of high school but I struck out in the relationship department as badly as Rex did. I kept liking boys who thought of me as a friend. Who wants a friend? I wanted someone to tell me I was pretty and smart and to buy me a Valentine's Day rose. The high school tradition was for the cheerleaders to deliver the Valentine's Day roses during class and I longed for that to happen to me.

I finally got my wish for a boyfriend when at 16, Tom asked me on a date. We knew each other from church youth activities and had passed in the hallways at school. Tom was in a different church congregation than me so we didn't worship together on Sundays. The first time we spoke, he was coming in one school door and I was going out the other. Mid-swing of the doors I shouted, "Hey, you have really pretty blue eyes."

He looked startled and then smiled. The next time we ran into each other, Tom stopped and struck up a conversation. You can never go wrong with a well-placed compliment. Dale Carnegie in "How to Win Friends and Influence People" was right. Once again, books taught me how to solve my problems, like how to get a boy to notice you.

Tom was a year younger than me. We were a couple through my junior and senior years. I was always careful to keep a firm separation between our relationship at school and at my house. When my family moved around the block from his, Tom never came over or called me at home.

I expanded my hours of freedom by getting up at 5 a.m. to jog before school with Tom. Occasionally Virginia was still up when my alarm went off to run. I waited in my room until she went to bed for the coast to be clear. Tom and I really did jog and that time was important to me. I could talk about whatever was happening without any pressure to get to class or be home. Tom was the first boy to tell me he loved me and I believed him. Unfortunately, I didn't know how to love him back. I kept a space between us, even as I wished I didn't. I saw the hell Virginia and Harley caused Emelia about her boyfriends and I didn't want that to happen to me. I kept Tom and everyone else I cared about away from my home life. Tom patiently tried to win my trust but I was too stuck in survivor mode to be anything more than a friendly companion. That was all I could handle and I knew Tom deserved better.

My best girlfriend in high school was Stephanie. We met in 8th grade during PE and became friends our freshman year. Stephanie was smart and took advanced classes, so the only class we ever shared was PE. She helped keep me sane by letting me hang out with her, letting some of her popularity rub off on me. She was a lot like my first best girlfriend, Leslie. They were both good girls and didn't add to the drama I already had in my life. I wasn't interested in rebelling or hanging out with kids who did drugs or alcohol. The last thing I needed was more problems. I craved people who were calm and predictable. I considered myself lucky to have two best girlfriends. I wrote letters to Leslie but she had no idea what my life was like. Virginia read all incoming and outgoing mail so I had to be careful with what I wrote.

I tried to get help dealing with my pain from home by talking to my teachers in high school. None caught my hints for conversation beyond their class. My junior year I served as an aide in the principal's office. While Stephanie was taking college algebra to prepare for going to a university, I ran errands around the school for an hour a day. I talked to the school secretary in the office during the quiet times. I thought she was listening like Mr. Gross did. She wasn't. After hearing a few stories of the craziness at my house, she referred me to a teacher who ran a therapy group for troubled students. I was insulted at her implication that I needed therapy. Didn't she understand I wasn't the problem? It was my parents that were crazy, not me. I got her message loud and clear. At the end of the semester I transferred out of being an office helper.

Meanwhile, I decided to investigate the therapy idea. Maybe someone would have a magic way I could get away from my parents. I was given a paper for Virginia to sign giving me permission to be excused from class once a week for group therapy to help me with my teenage-related difficulties. Virginia signed the paper but commented I better keep the family out of whatever problems I thought I was having. I remembered the lesson I learned the first year Rex and I were adopted about keeping family business within the family.

I was sitting in my 3rd grade class when the door opened and the principal came in. She asked to speak to the class and showed us a handful of colorful plastic miniature dinosaurs. She explained they were from an expensive display in one of the 2nd grade classrooms. Someone had stolen a lot of the dinosaurs and now the display was ruined. She asked us students to keep an eye out for them in case they were somewhere else in the building. Without hesitating, I eagerly raised my hand. The principal looked startled, but called on me. "Yes, what would you like to say?" she asked.

"My sister, Emelia has dinosaurs just like those in our bedroom," I cheerfully volunteered, not comprehending what I was saying.

"Your sister does? Where did she get them?" the principal questioned.

"I don't know. She said her teacher gave them to her," I replied.

The next thing I knew, I was out in the hallway with the principal and she asked me my sister's name, what class she was in and for a description of what the dinosaurs looked like.

I thought it was a bit weird, but it was nice that the principal thanked me for helping them out. I didn't give it another thought until I got home from school and was met by Virginia and Grandma Quigley at the door.

"Why did you tell the school Emelia had plastic dinosaurs in her room?" Virginia demanded.

I didn't answer.

"You had no business telling them anything. You should have waited until you got home and told us. We are her parents and it is our job to deal with problems, not the schools."

I nodded, not sure what to do. It honestly hadn't occurred to me that Emelia swiped the dinosaurs. I assumed her teacher let her have them, like she said. Later that evening, a family meeting was convened in the forbidden living room. I rubbed my palm across the plush couch cushion I sat on, marveling how soft it was. Other than to dust, we were so rarely allowed in the living room and never invited to sit on the furniture that anything in that room took on special significance.

Harley and Virginia took turns explaining to all of us kids that when things come up outside the family, we shouldn't volunteer any information to anyone until after we discuss it at home. Family business was no one else's concern but ours. We keep things in the family; we do not talk about our business in public. After we were lectured, everyone was dismissed to their rooms except Emelia. Before I could close the door to our shared bedroom, I heard the familiar whack from the stick as Emelia took her punishment. I felt a pang of regret sweep over me. I never should have said anything about the dinosaurs at school.

The first high school therapy session ran the same way they all would. We sat in a circle, about 10 kids and a PE teacher. Most of the kids I had never met. It was big school with over 3,000 students and it was entirely possible to go all four years there and never lay eyes on any of them.

We took turns introducing ourselves and then talking

about our week. I was told I didn't have to speak until I was comfortable. I attended group for several weeks, just listening to the others. They talked about being rebellious, fighting with their parents, drinking and taking drugs. Most of their problems seemed self-inflicted. I waited for someone to talk about abusive parents, but no one did. After a month of silently participating the teacher turned to me and asked when I was going to start sharing. He said it was fine if I didn't want to talk but that this group was formed to help students, not give them an excuse to get out of class. I felt helpless. What could I say? Where would I start? How much should I say? I didn't feel like I could trust these strangers with Rex, my years in foster care and my ongoing daily struggle to protect my spirit while living with people I despised. It seemed to me that no big help was going to come from talking. The teacher in charge of group didn't offer concrete help for anyone. He was just there to supervise the conversation. Talk about the blind leading the blind. I stopped attending soon after.

Virginia's family secrets stayed safe with me. I was in silent despair most of the time. I repeated my mantra, "I can do this. Only __ more years until I'm eighteen." My birthdays were not celebrations of my life, they were the official countdown of years to my escape.

10. MY TURN TO FLY

Two weeks before my high school graduation Virginia said I wasn't going to be allowed to attend the graduation ceremony. I was furious. I had already paid the $22 fee for my graduation cap and gown from my part-time job. Who forbids their kid from attending their own graduation? I had been grounded most of my senior year due to having a bad attitude. I hadn't done anything wrong; I just wasn't smiling when Virginia was around. It was exhausting living at home. It was like being a rat in a maze, not knowing when the next electric shock would come. It was definitely coming; it was just a matter of when.

When I explained my graduation dilemma to a couple of trusted women at church, they agreed to help. They cornered Virginia after Sunday services, asking her when my graduation was so they could attend. The social pressure of having to explain why I wouldn't be allowed to go to my own graduation was too great for Virginia and she rescinded my punishment that afternoon.

Virginia and Harley went to my graduation. Afterward Virginia complained about how hot it was, how long the program was and how they couldn't hear a thing. There was no graduation party for me at home. I was thrilled when they allowed me to attend Stephanie's party at her house. The graduation cake had both Stephanie's name and mine on it! What a wonderful surprise for me. Her parents wanted to make sure I had a graduation party.

After graduation, Stephanie proposed we take a road trip. She had a very cool classic Mustang car her Dad had restored for her. She was thinking of driving up the coast of California to the National Redwood Forest. I suggested we keep going north and revisit my childhood in Oregon. Of course, I had no money for a trip. At the very last minute, Harley and Virginia gave me $100 towards the trip as a graduation gift. Stephanie and her Dad paid for the rest of the trip. My only other contribution was my sparkling personality.

I was dazzled when Stephanie came to pick me up for our trip and I was actually allowed to go. I expected Virginia, at the very last minute, to forbid me from going. I don't think she remembered I was leaving. After she agreed I could go, I never mentioned the trip again at home. The morning Stephanie came to get me, Virginia was still asleep and Harley was gone to work. I slipped out as quietly as I could, whispering a goodbye to Grandma Quigley, who was watching The Price is Right in her room. As Stephanie cleared the end of our block and I was certain Virginia wasn't coming after me, I breathed a sigh of relief. For the first time in ten years, I was free. Instead of collapsing, the feeling of lightness filled me like a balloon. I was high on life and began talking at manic speed to Stephanie. Poor Stephanie! I talked non-stop for hours and hours. It was enlivening to be away from the oppressiveness of the Spencers.

Stephanie drove from Phoenix to the Pacific Ocean, then up the coast of California, ending up in Eugene, Oregon. She checked in with her parents at least once a day, letting them know we were ok and where we were. We stayed a few days with my grade school girlfriend, Leslie and her parents. Seeing Leslie and her parents after seven years felt natural to me, as if I had never left. It was an odd feeling to stay in the house I so vividly imagined living in years before. I was living my fantasy and it was nice. Stephanie, Leslie and I took a lot of pictures together. I was so happy introducing the two friends who independently from each other, made me feel accepted in the same way.

The only time I called home during the trip was from

Leslie's kitchen phone. Her mother insisted my folks would be worried after a week of not hearing from me. I reluctantly made the call with Leslie's family and Stephanie listening as Virginia yelled about how long I had been gone, the kitchen was a mess and I had responsibilities to take care of. The call ended with me in tears, vowing to get out of their house as soon as possible. Leslie's mom was shaken by Virginia's response and apologized for wanting me to call home. Stephanie and Leslie didn't say anything. What was there to say?

Stephanie, Leslie and I took a day trip from Eugene to Portland. I wanted to visit Rex, Ralph and Claudia. I didn't call ahead to arrange a visit because I was fearful of what kind of weirdness I would be walking into with my friends. All I really wanted to know was that Rex was ok. I didn't prepare either of my friends for what we might encounter in Portland because I wasn't sure of what I actually knew about my biological family. Did Claudia really have schizophrenia or was that something I made up as a kid? Was Ralph really unable to take care of children or did he have a more sinister problem? I didn't know and I was as nervous as a cat on a hot tin roof as we drove to Portland.

As we drove up to the address I had for Ralph and Claudia, I was surprised at the door by Claudia's mother, Lennis. I didn't remember her. The only baby photo I had was a picture of her holding me outside a house. On the back was scrawled in pen, "Haddie with Grandma Lennis Brown." Lennis burst into tears when she realized who I was. Other than her hair was grayish white, she looked remarkably the same, down to her cat-eye glasses. She looked disheveled and worn, just like the rest of the house. Claudia and Rex weren't home and Lennis didn't know when they would be back. She complained it was difficult having Rex around because all he liked to do was sit and read comic books. I was comforted when Lennis showed me a picture of Rex. He had grown significantly and put on weight. He looked very good compared to his years living with the Spencers. From the picture I knew going to Oregon was the right choice for Rex.

We got directions from Lennis to the Lloyd shopping center where Ralph worked as a dishwasher. I remembered riding the city bus as a small child to visit Ralph at work. It was shocking to realize he was still doing the same job fifteen years later.

When we got to the restaurant I approached the manager with a handshake, saying, "Hi, I'm Heather Spencer and I was wondering if I could visit with Ralph Wade? I'm his daughter."

The manager hesitated, saying something about it being a busy lunchtime. The dining room didn't look very busy to me. Stephanie stepped up and said, "Ralph hasn't seen his daughter in years. What would it hurt to take a few minutes to visit?"

I was grateful for her boldness because my heart was beating out of my chest. The manager grunted and opened the kitchen door, yelling, "Hey Ralph, your daughter is here to see you."

Ralph's back was turned to the doorway. He was about my height with dark brown hair that curled up against his shirt collar. I could see his hands plunged into a sink full of suds.

His head jerked up, and he growled, "Whadda want now?" over his shoulder.

The manger yelled again, "Ralph, your daughter is here to see you. Hurry it up!"

Ralph stopped washing and turned around to face his boss. "My daughter? What are you talking about?"

I poked my head into the doorway and said, "Hi, Ralph. How are you?"

He stared at me for a moment and squealed, "Hey, it's my daughter! What are you doing here? I didn't know you were coming. No one told me."

He quickly dried his hands and skated across the wet kitchen floor to me. "You sure are pretty."

He turned to his boss and said, "Isn't she pretty?"

Ralph smiled and I could see crooked teeth under his bushy moustache. The manger turned away from us and said, "You got fifteen minutes and then get back to work. This isn't visiting hour."

We all went into an empty dining room, where Stephanie took pictures of Ralph and me. Ralph kept staring at me as if I were a ghost. Our 15 minutes were quickly devoured. I regretted not having more time with him. Ralph was genuinely thrilled to see me and it felt really good. Soon enough his boss appeared, telling Ralph to get back to the dishes. I was annoyed since the mostly deserted restaurant didn't seem to have a pressing need for plates. I felt sorry Ralph had to work for such a jerk.

After our visit in Oregon, Stephanie and I continued our road trip without seeing Claudia or Rex. I was fine with not seeing Rex and Claudia. Rex looked good in the pictures and Claudia felt like a strange, scary image from long ago memories. We stopped in Las Vegas before heading back to Phoenix. Two weeks away wasn't nearly enough for me.

Back at home Virginia demanded to know why we didn't continue north from Oregon and go visit Harley's parents in Washington State. I never planned on going to Washington. I explained that by the time we got to Oregon our money was running out and Stephanie said we needed to go home. Virginia said, "If you went to your grandparents they would have given you money to finish your trip. Once again, you were selfish and it was all about what you want, not thinking of anyone else."

The facts that Stephanie's family paid for the entire trip, which turned out to be not a carefree celebration of youth but instead a weird half-reunion with my childhood, and that I had no idea Virginia told grandparents I barely knew to expect us, escaped her. When I returned home from the road trip, I knew the time was drawing close for me to find a way out.

Over the years with Virginia and Harley I saw a pattern of them attracting and collecting broken, desperate people who were already adults. I have no idea how many of them where actually legally adopted by them. I watched as Virginia and Harley accepted Wanda, a single mother with a small child, then Steve, a 22 year-old guy who ended up going to prison for being a sexual predator, and then Eugene Columbaro. He was a divorced thirty- something year-old father with children of his own. The Spencers welcomed messed up people like a crazy lady hoards cats.

When I was a sophomore in high school, Eugene babysat his girlfriend Joyce's son while she was at work. The boy was 6 year-old Adam Clark, who had Cornelia De Lang Syndrome, a rare genetic disability that left him unable to walk, talk or care for himself. Adam died under Eugene's care. Murder charges were brought against Eugene alleging he caused the child's death by throwing him against a wall and hitting him.

Emelia and I were called to testify in court on Eugene's behalf. I saw Eugene's fiery temper with his ex-wife and how rude he was to his own children. I knew Eugene was not a patient person and that Adam was completely dependent on others to meet his needs. There was no way Eugene had the loving temperament that child needed. Adam communicated by squeals, grunts and cries. You had to pay close attention to figure out what he needed. I only babysat Adam a few times and found the experience completely stressful. I testified in court that the boy had terrible temper tantrums and had thrown himself on the floor and hit himself when I babysat him. It made me sick to have to testify for Eugene. No one, not Eugene's lawyer or the prosecuting lawyer asked me if I thought it was possible for Eugene to cause harm to the child. I couldn't prove it but I knew in my heart he did it.

After Eugene was found not guilty of murder and released, his lawyer congratulated and thanked me. My composed, calm testimony was crucial in getting Eugene found innocent. My stomach hurt after I was told my testimony was a factor in Eugene walking away. Years later, the original detective on the case found new evidence and Eugene was charged once again with the child's death. This time he was found guilty and served time in prison. It was late and not nearly enough jail time, but a tiny bit of justice was served for little Adam Clark.

During the time of charging Eugene with murder and his trial, Eugene legally changed his name to Harley Debbs Spencer II so he could claim at least in name, to be related to my adoptive parents. Harley wasn't happy about Eugene taking his name but he and Virginia both fully believed in Eugene's innocence and grieved Joyce's son's death as if their own grandchild had passed.

Since it wouldn't be right for Eugene to babysit Joyce's preteen daughter by himself while she worked, Virginia and Joyce thought it would be a great idea if I moved into Joyce's apartment and helped her care of her remaining daughter. I wanted nothing to do with Eugene, Joyce or her son's death. The whole thing was incredibly sad and I could not understand why Virginia and Harley continued to insist Eugene was a member of the family. I had to get away from the Spencers and anyone they considered family.

A month before my 18th birthday I got into an argument with Virginia and stormed out of the house. That was the first time with the Spencers that I openly rebelled. I spent the night with Tom's family. I decided I had had enough and was leaving.

I went back the next morning to get my stuff and found Virginia awake and furious. She grabbed me, slapped my face and shoved me against the wall, telling me if I left the house again she would call the police because I was still a minor. I was banished to my room. The following Wednesday I met with the bishop. Virginia allowed me to leave the house only because she thought the bishop would chastise me for my behavior. The bishop listened to my story and sadly agreed I had to stay with my parents but only until I was eighteen. He told me to hang in there until my birthday and after that, I was free to leave with his best wishes.

I knew from Virginia's reaction to my attempt to leave that she would not allow me to just waltz out the door. I prayed for days to find a way to leave peacefully. Both Harley and Virginia scared the crap out of me and I didn't want another confrontation with either of them.

My birthday that year was on a Saturday. On Friday afternoon, my miracle from God happened. Harley and Virginia never went anywhere. They didn't take trips or go out for an evening. Virginia didn't even sit outside in the yard. She spent her life moving between her bed and recliner. Virginia hardly went to church anymore, preferring to stay at home with Grandma Quigley while Harley, Matthew and I went to services.

When I got home from work the day before my birthday they were preparing for a weekend getaway. Harley announced they would be gone overnight and would be home on Saturday evening. That truly was a miracle. I packed my boxes and bright and early Saturday morning Tom brought his truck and helped me load my stuff. I gave Grandma Quigley the address and phone number of where I was going so Virginia couldn't say I ran away. I was 18 years-old and they couldn't make me stay. I intended to never go back.

I had four different families who offered to take me in. Mr. Gross and his wife, Carol, with whom I maintained a relationship since junior high, were the first to suggest I live with them. I also got invitations from Stephanie's parents, my boyfriend's parents and the Bingham family. I thought of the pros and cons of each situation. I loved that so many people wanted me and I was worried about offending someone by not taking their generous offer, but I needed a specific kind of situation. I had an unreliable car to get me around town and my new part-time job didn't pay enough for me to afford a better one. I had to live on the bus route to get to my job in case my car wouldn't start. I also wanted a permanent place, not a temporary bed. I was terrified if I couldn't live on my own I might end up back at the Spencers, trapped forever. In the end I decided to go with the Bingham family. They were members of the Mormon Church and I wanted to stay active in that faith.

Being Mormon was a conscious choice I made at 17. For years Harley and Virginia harangued all of us kids about reading the scriptures, especially The Book of Mormon. Because of their non-stop preaching about it, I wasn't interested in ever reading that book. My senior year of high school, the Mormon religion class I attended during the school day as an elective course was formally studying The Book of Mormon. I took the teacher's challenge to read it. It was silly that I hadn't read it previously since I was reading at least two books a week in my spare time. Once I took Harley and Virginia out of the mental equation, I breezed through the book in less than a week. In the last chapter of the book, I read Moroni 10:4.

"And when ye shall receive these things, I would exhort you that ye would ask God, the Eternal Father, in the name of Christ, if these things are not true; and if ye shall ask with a sincere heart, with real intent, having faith in Christ, he will manifest the truth of it unto you, by the power of the Holy Ghost."

This verse created an unexpected problem for me. I was reading the book to check it off my list of 'Things Good People Do.' I hadn't predicted the force it would hit me with. Pray and ask if this was true? And what if it wasn't? Then what?

Although I had good friends outside of the Mormon church, like Stephanie and Mr. Gross, I hadn't talked to any of them about my faith. It was my religion class instructor, Brother Davis, who told me Heavenly Father loved me enough that He wouldn't want me chasing after stupid boys who would never see beyond my bad clothes and pimples. Brother Davis was my moral father-figure who protected my reputation and steered me away from those who would get me into irreparable trouble.

Brother Davis believed in being Mormon and he said he believed the Book of Mormon was true. If he said it was true, wasn't that good enough for me? I didn't want to take the challenge the scripture invited. I didn't want to have to choose

111

another path if it was wrong. Where would I go, who would comfort me, and where would I find God if not in the Mormon faith?

While I was in foster care I didn't pick any of the churches I attended. I have no idea how many of them I was baptized into. I definitely didn't get to pick my faith after being adopted. After adoption I didn't even get to choose what I wore to church. According to Virginia and Harley, God expected me to dress like a lady for church whether I liked it or not.

I pondered for days the possible outcomes from praying about the Book of Mormon. I didn't tell anyone what I was thinking about. I didn't want to be talked into believing The Book of Mormon. I didn't want to be talked out of it, either. I just needed to know what God wanted me to do.

I always believed there was a God. The world seemed silly and hopeless if there wasn't something beyond my mortal experience. I could not accept that I had lived through such a crappy childhood with no real vision of a better adulthood. Surely there had to be a bigger purpose than just survival. All my anxiety, loneliness and fear had to count for something to someone. No matter what church I sat in, what biblical coloring page I traced, or hymn I tried to sing, I had always assumed God was there. Why wouldn't He be in church just like I was?

After days of thinking, fighting back wave after wave of my fear of the unknown, I finally gave in. The devil I didn't know was going to unveil himself one way or another. I sat in the chapel pew on Sunday, the congregation quiet around me as the Sacrament was being passed down the pews. In the collective silence I took a deep breath, closed my eyes and said the most sincere internal prayer of my life. "Is the Book of Mormon true? Is this where I should put my faith?" The answer came at me instantaneously from all directions, dazzling me with a lightness and warmth that filled my body with a physical sensation of pure joy. For me, God wanted me to know the Book of Mormon was true.

I knew when I moved out of the Spencer's house, I needed to find people who understood my faith and would support it. I met Vernon and Anna Bingham through my friendship with their son. Our freshman year Mike and I shared Brother Davis's religion class and a couple of other classes so we naturally fell into step together. The Bingham's had eight children, but only Mike still lived at home. Anna reminded me of Leslie's mother. Whenever I managed to sneak out to visit the Binghams, Anna always had food in the refrigerator and welcomed me to eat whatever I wanted in the kitchen. I didn't have to ask permission, something that was unimaginable in my adoptive home. The best part was although they lived less than three miles from the Spencers, they attended services in a different building so I knew I would never have to cross paths with Harley or Virginia at church.

I knew if I stayed with my boyfriend Tom and his family it would only be temporary. They lived around the corner from the Spencers and attended the same congregation at church. Besides, no self-respecting Mormon family would let their teenaged son's girlfriend move in permanently. The scandal at church would be too much and I knew it wouldn't be fair to put them through the turmoil. The Binghams met all my criteria, including my need for public transportation when my crappy car broke down, which was often.

Before they offered to let me stay with them, the Binghams counseled with their Bishop and Stake President at church about my situation. After much thought, they decided to take a chance on me.

Within a week of my leaving, Virginia called the Bingham house at 5 a.m. She told Anna I was a liar because I left and didn't tell them. I was a thief because I took a full length mirror from my bedroom. And finally, Virginia crowed, she had proof the only reason I wanted to live with the Binghams was to get pregnant by their son, Mike.

I was humiliated by that last part and felt very unsure of

my standing with the Binghams.

While I was learning how to be Mormon in the Spencers house, I was taught in church that everyone should have a journal. Writing in a journal was a way to remember God's blessings and provided a record of my life for future generations. I loved the idea of writing my story. I carefully printed my name inside the cover and drew a picture of myself on the first page. I thought my someday great-great-grandchildren would be curious to know what I looked like. I drew a happy face with shoulder length, pencil stringed hair that barely covered my skull. It was a perfect 8 year-old rendition of me. I don't remember what I wrote next, but that was the beginning of my habit of journal writing. By the time I left the Spencers, I had a whole shelf of journals in my bedroom. For some reason that makes no sense now, I thought my journals were private, not subject to Virginia's prying eyes. I told the truth in my journals. I wrote about boys I thought were cute, my teachers in school and even recorded the more heinous acts of abuse Harley and Virginia heaped on Rex and my adoptive siblings. I didn't have any spiritual experiences to write about. I had long forgotten the original point of journal writing. I did it because it felt like a safe way for me to vent my stream of constant resentment toward the Spencer's. I liked to write and it made me feel better. I didn't realize until I moved in with the Binghams that Virginia stole at least one of my journals. It was from when I was 14 and wrote in girly, swirly script "I Love Mike Bingham" over who knows how many pages of my half-sized journal.

The first week of high school I realized I shared almost half of my classes with Mike Bingham. I saw him all day long in school. When he showed up in my elective Mormon religion class, I realized he was Mormon just like me. It didn't take long for us to start talking and we became friends. Mike was cute and soon I had random girls asking if he was my boyfriend because we walked together in the halls and often ate lunch together.

One morning before school Mike and I were standing

around shooting the breeze and a cheerleader came up to Mike. She interrupted our conversation by asking, "So what's the deal with you two? She (pointing to me) can't possibly be your girlfriend, so is she your sister?"

I was stunned into silence when Mike flung his arm over my shoulder and said, "Yes. Heather is my sister."

The cheerleader smiled and walked away, throwing "I thought so" over her shoulder. Mike pulled me in close and whispered in my ear, "That will get them talking, won't it?"

I enjoyed the attention of being friends with a popular boy. It was my first time to be considered part of the cool kids club. I still wore thrift store clothes and ate government subsidized free lunches, but Mike didn't seem to care about that. It didn't take long for me to develop a full blown case of puppy love. Who wouldn't? Mike not only listened to me and laughed at my jokes, sometimes he even gave me a ride home on the handlebars of his BMX bike. Of course, like all red-blooded teenage girls do, I documented in my journals every breathless event that proved my feelings of adoration were justified. It didn't take long into my friendship with Mike before he confided his undying love for a girl who attended a different school. When I realized the depth of Mike's feelings, I knew I didn't have a chance. Who could compete with the kind of beauty he saw in the girl of his dreams? Not me. Mike's girl wore real Levi's with a tiny red tag on the back pocket and genuine leather Nike tennis shoes. I wore knock-offs from the Factory-To-U store and hand stitched designs on my plain jean back pockets. No competition here.

Mike and I kept our friendship throughout high school, even as he transferred to another school and I no longer saw him in my classes. I appreciated his non-judgmental attitude about my looks and thrift store clothes. Our long-standing high school friendship paid off when I was looking for a way out the Spencer's house.

During the physical altercation I had with Virginia before I moved out, she said something to me that jolted me into reality. She quoted a paragraph I had written in my journal where I called her my personal Mommy Dearest. It was a reference to a book written by Joan Crawford's daughter about her abusive childhood. In that moment, it all became clear. Virginia read my journals. I had no idea how much she read or when. She had never tipped her hand before about reading them and that is why I lulled myself into believing my journals were safe. I was horrified and worried that she would use my words against me. I also wanted to know what she thought of entry after entry that I wrote over the years describing how badly she and Harley treated Rex. Did she feel any remorse? Did it help her see herself for the monster she was? I couldn't imagine any way for me to ask those questions without bringing her rage down on me, but I took satisfaction in knowing I wrote it all down. She should feel nothing but ashamed of herself. I gathered up all my journals and threw them in the garbage can in the alley behind our house. That was all I could do. I no longer had any record of my life for my great-great-great grandchildren to read. I hoped God would understand.

The journal Virginia stole came back to haunt me. She called Anna Bingham at the crack of dawn every morning and read my words to her. My face burned with shame and regret when Anna quietly asked me if I had feelings for her son. My life was hanging in the balance. What could I possibly say to Mrs. Bingham that would convince her to let me stay? I had no choice but to tell the truth. Yes, when I first met her son, I did have a crush on him. He was the first boy who was nice to me. But that quickly faded into a genuine feeling of friendship, not romance. When I finished my humiliating confession I waited for her response, praying she wouldn't ask me to leave. I had nowhere to go and no money to get there. She didn't say anything, she just nodded and picked up the morning newspaper.

I held my breath the rest of the day, pushing my panic down as I waited for Vernon to get home from work and for Anna to tell him what I had admitted about their son. I tiptoed around quietly, expecting to be called to a formal meeting with Vernon. I was willing to be embarrassed again by repeating my confession to Mike's father. No one said a word. I decided that night that I was probably safe, as long as I was careful to never, ever give off the I Like Your Son vibe.

I have to give full credit to Anna. She put up with the telephone harassment for a week before telling Virginia to stop calling. They didn't kick me out and there was no pressure to go back to the Spencers. I was furious at Virginia for the things she said about me, especially the accusation I had romantic intentions towards Mike. It felt as awkward as I imagined it would have been if I had stayed with Tom and his family. I also knew Anna was hearing gossip at church about the wisdom of having a teenage girl living in her house while their son still lived at home. The whole thing was mortifying and I wanted to crawl into a hole. All I needed was a safe place to land. That was all.

My other tests with the Binghams came very quickly. Just a few days into living in their house, while I was still feeling fragile and very much like a guest, I found myself in a terrible situation. It was one that in the Spencers home I hadn't faced in years because I always made sure I was prepared. I was in the hall bathroom and after having finished my personal business, I was horrified to discover there was no toilet paper. I didn't know what to do and more importantly, didn't have any money to solve the problem. I managed to take care of my immediate problem with scraps from the nearby trash can but I didn't know what to do next. Do I ask for paper? What if they get mad? Will they throw me out? Where will I go next? I really wanted to stay, but knew based on previous life experience that everyone needs to carry his or her own weight.

After stewing for an hour I found the courage to bring up the topic. Anna and Vernon were sitting in the family room, watching tv. I waited for a commercial and then hesitantly asked, "Um, do you guys have any toilet paper I could borrow until I get paid again?"

They looked at me for a moment and Anna asked, "Why

would you need to borrow toilet paper?"

I explained that I didn't have any money at the time to buy my own toilet paper and that I would pay them back as soon as I could. She laughed and said, "Oh honey, the paper goods are in the storage room. You don't have to buy anything here. We provide that for everyone. You don't need to worry about that. The soap and shampoo is also in on the shelf."

A few days later I overheard Anna talking on the phone, telling someone else about the toilet paper incident and the conversation ended with her saying, "Honestly! Who ever heard of not putting paper in the bathroom? Those people sure are sickos. No wonder Heather is like a jack rabbit, afraid of her own shadow."

That was the beginning of my training of what normal family life was like. I was ecstatic to be assigned to only one household chore, keeping the hall bathroom clean. That was it. I washed my own clothes, but only because I preferred to. Anna would have done my laundry along with Vernon's and Mike's but no way was I going to take advantage of her hospitality. I admit a part of me was proud I was more self-sufficient than Mike was.

Other new adventures unfolded naturally as I watched how Mike got food out of fridge without asking, used the phone without being monitored and even occasionally smart-mouthed his parents with no repercussions. It was amazing to watch. For the first time in my life I experienced what it felt like to relax.

I broke up with Tom. He was still in high school and I was enrolled in the local community college. After leaving the Spencers, I was anxious to put my old life behind me and I wanted to be free to date others. I felt terrible about it because Tom had been such a loyal boyfriend and had never pressured me to have sex or do anything inappropriate. He deserved someone who could reciprocate his affections.

I started dating with reckless abandon. It was so great to flirt and have the attention of the opposite sex. Unfortunately, I wasn't very good at picking possible suitors. I wanted exciting, daring and adventurous. What I got instead was a string of scary, questionable, mentally-ill types that made the Binghams wonder what kind of person I really was. Why would I be interested in boys who gave me notes threatening their suicide? What happened to the nice boy I dated in high school? I dated quite a variety of losers, more than I could have imagined were available. Vernon and Anna both talked to me separately about who I was spending time with. Anna said they were praying for me. Even Mike got in the on the action, telling me straight out he didn't like a particular boy I brought home. While I should have had my head examined for the reckless, drama-filled boys I was hanging around with, I was secretly thrilled the Binghams cared enough to talk to me about my choices. It touched me that they considered me worthy of their prayers.

I talked on the phone openly in front of the family and gave my new home phone number to my friends. Mail came to the house with my name on it and I was allowed to take it without it first being read or having to ask permission. Once I even invited some of my friends over to watch a movie. I was wound up tight before my friends came but when it was over I considered my first party a success.

I tried to not be a burden on Anna. I didn't have much money from my part-time job and the money I did make went to keeping the crappy car I bought insured and running. One night I offered to cook dinner. It was my first attempt cooking for someone other than the Spencers. I was used to cooking large amounts of food and greatly overshot the mark. It became the first thing the Binghams could gently tease me about, 'feeding the 5,000.'

I grew very quickly to love leftovers. They were easy to heat in the microwave, Vernon and Mike didn't like them so they were always there, waiting for me to eat. Anna was a great cook and everything always tasted even better on the second day. My hair that had been hopelessly thin all my life, began growing thick and full. In the fall when I went to visit Mr. Gross in his library, he commented on how shiny my hair was and how clear my complexion was. He was happy I was doing so well. I enjoyed his compliment.

Every night there was food prepared for dinner and I didn't have to make it. Every morning when I got up Anna was sitting at the kitchen table, reading the newspaper after getting Vernon off to work. She was pleasant and would ask about my plans for the day. I felt like I was living in a modern "Brady Bunch" episode. After a short while in their house I started calling them Mom and Dad like Mike did and no one objected.

The Binghams helped me when my car was broken, which it was most of the time. Occasionally they would drive me where I needed to go. I didn't ask for rides very often, sensitive to not overstretch my welcome. For my first Christmas with them, Mom Bingham bought me perfume and a large make-up kit. I began experimenting with being a woman, buying clothes from the mall and trying for the first time to look my best. Mom complimented and encouraged my efforts. Dad and Mike good-naturedly teased me about being on a man hunt. I basked in all their attention. I was feeling loved.

The only thing that was hard for me while living with the Binghams was the intense jealousy I felt deep inside of me when all their grown children and grandchildren came over. It was all was so happy and perfect compared to the foster home and the Spencers. I desperately wanted to be a part of it, not just Mom and Dad's latest social project.

They had helped other troubled kids in years past, thus my presence wasn't an entirely new experience for the family. Mom Bingham introduced me to others as their foster daughter, which was a nice way to say she had taken in a stray. They had no idea that for me being called a foster kid was loaded with all kinds of baggage. Like Rex, I just wanted a real family of my very own. A forever family. Theirs was the first family I met that I wanted to be a part of and who made me feel special and loved.

After living with the Binghams for a year I met and began dating a guy named Rob. I met him at a Young Adult Dance held in a local church gym, the equivalent of a Mormon matchmaking party. Since active church members don't drink alcohol or smoke, the bar scene isn't the best place for Mormons to go if looking for love. I knew Rob's family but hadn't met him. He had just returned home from serving a church mission in Southern Mexico. He was still in missionary mode and wasn't dancing or talking to any girls in the gym. He had spent 18 months focused on preaching the gospel in Spanish and hadn't yet flipped back into the reality of America. During our first dance he admitted he asked me to dance because I was the only girl wearing a dress that night. He thought that made me seem safer than the rest of the girls who were wearing jeans. I didn't have the heart to tell him I was only wearing a dress because I didn't have time to change after work. It had nothing to do with my piety. Shortly after our introduction at the dance, Rob asked me out on a date.

Mom and Dad Bingham loved Rob when he showed up in a dress shirt and tie and was shyly polite to them. They were vocal about other boys I had brought home that didn't fit their standards. Rob was a breath of fresh air for them. He and I dated casually for six months. He was determined to get the first college degree in his family. I understood there was no immediate future with him. I dated him strictly because he was cute and I enjoyed the movies and dances we went to. At the end of the summer, we parted ways.

I transferred to Northern Arizona University in the fall, living on student loans and a part-time job. My dorm roommate was on a full-ride scholarship that paid for everything. I couldn't afford the mandatory cafeteria plan for eating, which turned out to not be so mandatory if you didn't have money for it. I had $20 a week budgeted for food. I ate an ice cream bar from the vending machine for breakfast, an apple for lunch and a frozen burrito heated up in my toaster oven for dinner. Occasionally my privileged roommate shared a piece of her pizza with me. She complained about gaining the freshman 15 lbs. while my weight plummeted. My once tight size three jeans hung on my waist and my teeth loosened in my mouth. Worried, I bought a bottle of vitamins to help myself. I had vivid dreams about grocery shopping and finding money scattered on the store floor, with me scrambling to pick up the change before anyone could stop me. I was once again in survival mode.

I ran into Rob at a regional church dance. I ended up spending the evening with Rob, ignoring the boy who graciously drove three hours to take me to the dance. The evening ended with Rob escorting me to the car in the parking lot where my fuming driver was impatiently waiting. He had assumed it was clear we were on a date, I thought we were friends sharing a ride. Oops. It was a long, silent ride back to campus at 1 a.m. I couldn't apologize enough, the damage was done. My driver/date told everyone who would listen that I was the biggest flirt on campus.

After that night, Rob was smitten. I do have to admit, I looked good at the dance. I wore a pink cashmere sweater that Leslie sent me as a Christmas present in high school. It was my good luck sweater because I always wore it for job interviews and felt confident in it. My magic sweater certainly worked with Rob. He started driving the three hours from his parents' house in Phoenix to the NAU campus in Flagstaff on the weekends to visit. We talked on the phone almost every night. There is a price for romance and I couldn't afford it. My long-distance phone bill was over $300 for the month of November. My "scrambling for money" dreams got more intense.

When Rob realized he was getting serious about me, he talked to Mom and Dad Bingham and asked their advice. They told him what I was like when I first moved in. I was a mess, they explained to Rob. I had vivid nightmares of the Spencers and slept walked. They never knew where I was going to end up. I cried, moaned and talked in my sleep. They told Rob if he had known me then he would not have been interested in me. It is amazing what unconditional love can heal and I love the Binghams for giving me that.

Rob also went to the former bishop of the church

congregation I attended during my teenage years. Rob had heard my side of the family story and plenty of rumors from others. He wanted to make sure I wasn't a psycho chick like the rest of the Spencers. He explained his situation to the bishop and asked him his opinion of my family and me. Normally the bishop is bound by confidentiality in all matters related to members of the congregation but it had been years since my family lived in his congregation and he was no longer serving as bishop. He felt Rob had the right to know what he was getting into.

The bishop told Rob about the evening my parents and Emelia came to his office. When Harley and Virginia found out Emelia was pregnant at 16 they threw a big fit. Emelia stormed out of the house and didn't come back for a few weeks. She stayed at her boyfriend's house. After she returned they took her to the bishop hoping he would talk some sense into her. Virginia and Harley wanted her to break up with her boyfriend, stay at home during her pregnancy and then give the baby up for adoption, along with a healthy dose of punishment for her sins. Only Emelia didn't want that. She and her boyfriend planned on getting married and she wanted Harley and Virginia to give their legal permission since she was underage.

The bishop explained to the Spencers that they couldn't control Emelia. The church's official position was that if the father was willing to marry and support the child, the couple should get married. This was Emelia's decision to make and it was their job to be loving, supportive and to figure out how to be helpful to her and her new husband. Harley stood up in a rage, grabbed the bishop by the front of his shirt and told him that there was no way in hell that was going to happen. The bishop explained to Rob that before that incident there was plenty of evidence that things were not right at our house but that was the first time in his life he ever felt threatened by anyone. He told Rob out of everyone in the family, I was the only sane one and it was safe to believe whatever I told him. He also told Rob not to worry about dating or marrying me. I was fine and a good girl.

All along Rob kept telling me he liked me but that marriage was out of the question until he got his degree. That was at least three years away. I was fine with dating, if I could figure out a way to pay for it. I really liked Rob but I understood his dilemma. I didn't have any money and neither did he. I had been burned enough by crazy boys that I wasn't about to put my heart into a relationship that was tenuous at best. Lastly, I didn't want to have the reputation of being on a Husband Hunt. Nothing was socially worse than appearing to want to get married. At the same time, being good Mormons, getting married is exactly what was expected. Mormon college congregations are designed for dating, courting and marrying. Living together or having premarital sex was unthinkably taboo. The unspoken rules of the dating game were just so complicated. I just wanted one stable guy I could count on.

On the first weekend in December Rob came to visit me. We ate at Denny's on Friday night, which I was grateful for. The only time I got a full meal was when Rob fed me. After we ate we went back to the apartment he was staying at. With trembling hands, Rob produced a ring box. I was surprised. For a guy who protested he didn't want to get married, he was moving fast. In what can only be described as the work of angels, I managed to keep quiet and let Rob speak first. Good thing I did. He showed me a simple gold band with intertwining hearts and a tiny diamond chip in the center. He once again reminded me he was in no position to marry, but that he was offering me an exclusive friendship. Would I consider being his friend? Accepting the ring would mean we would date, but with no other long-term attachments until after college graduation. I was smiling so big my mouth almost cracked. I was laughing on the inside but I didn't want to hurt Rob's sincere attempt at landing his first ever girlfriend. He was trying so hard to be true to his heart and his head at the same time. I happily accepted the deal. After we parted for the evening, I went back to my dorm and showed all the girls on the floor my official friendship ring. Everyone was very confused as to its meaning. They had all lost their virginity long before, so Rob's gesture was puzzling and yet sweet. Our old-fashioned purity rules seemed archaic to them.

For the next 24 hours as Rob and I hung out on campus, I proudly showed off my new ring. I explained each time that it signified Rob's and my friendship. We weren't engaged, far from it. We were Official Friends. The girls in my student congregation at church were happy for me because that meant I was off the dating market.

Rob and I attended church together on Sunday morning. During the opening hymn of "Hark! The Herald Angels Sing" Rob leaned over and whispered in my ear, "Will you marry me?"

I didn't immediately reply. I thought, "What? We just became friends!"

We continued singing until the last stanza of the song. I quickly considered what being engaged and married meant. I leaned over and whispered in his ear, "Yes."

He looked at me and while closing the hymn book he responded, "Oh shoot."

The church service began and we sat together in silence, pondering what had just happened. I wondered what the "Oh shoot" was about. Did he make a mistake in proposing? Did he want to take it back? What was I supposed to do? I stewed for half an hour and couldn't stand it any longer. I leaned over and whispered, "What did you mean, "Oh shoot? Did you make a mistake?"

Rob put his arm around my shoulders and whispered back, "No! I wanted to ask you, but not like this. I wanted to wait and do something really neat. I just felt compelled to ask today and now I have ruined my chance. Now I will be stuck forever with this."

I smiled and he gave my shoulders a squeeze. The Word of God never sounded sweeter than that day.

When I called and told the Binghams I accepted Rob's proposal of marriage, they were thrilled, especially Dad

Bingham. From the very beginning he didn't do a good job hiding how much he like Rob, sometimes even more than he liked me.

Rob's parents weren't so excited when we broke the news to them. They knew the Spencers, they heard the stories over the years and they were concerned their son was marrying a girl with major baggage. It didn't get better when I explained about Ralph and Claudia, either. They were worried about their future grandchildren being born with disabilities and didn't want that burden for Rob. They were cordial to me, reserving their objections to our impending marriage for private conversations with their son. In the end, they reluctantly accepted Rob's decision and were supportive at our wedding.

While we were engaged Rob worried he would need to work full-time to support us and how that would affect his ability to get an education. I withdrew from school during winter break and moved back to the Binghams so I could work full-time and save money for our wedding. I did the best I could to reassure him I would help and that nothing would get in the way of him obtaining his university degree. I had absolutely no idea how I would help other than being by his side to solve problems as they came up. Rob and I got married just before my 20th birthday. He was 22 years-old and seemed so mature and worldly. Most importantly, he was patient with my $500 Chevy Nova and didn't get angry when I called repeatedly asking for a tow because it died in another busy intersection in downtown Phoenix. A man who can handle crap cars is worth a million dollars. I was grateful for his willingness to rescue me when I was drowning in an ocean of poverty, loneliness and fear. I knew women who had married for much, much less.

Out of a sense of social obligation I invited Harley and Virginia to the wedding. I was sick at the thought of them attending, but felt inviting them was the right thing to do. The Bingham family was naturally involved with my wedding and I was thrilled with their support.

I got a call at 5 a.m. the morning of our wedding from Emelia saying that Harley and Virginia were waiting for my call to invite them. I had mailed them an invitation and talked about the details of the wedding with them on the phone. The idea they needed another formal invitation smacked of manipulation and I wasn't going to do it. I was on pins and needles the whole day through the wedding ceremony, afternoon luncheon and evening reception, waiting for the other shoe to drop with unwanted drama. Other than tongues wagging all day about my absent adoptive family, nothing happened. My wedding photos are lovely and I am proud of the photo of Rob and I surrounded by the whole pack of Binghams representing my family. I mailed a wedding invitation to the last address I had for Rex, not knowing if he still lived in Oregon or if he would even get my letter. I didn't hear back from him.

I paid for most of our $700 wedding myself from the money I earned from my job as a sales clerk at an upscale department store. I didn't make enough during our six month engagement to save much but at least we didn't go into debt for the wedding. On our wedding day, between the two of us, we had $300 to our names. We were too poor to elope and we desperately needed the gifts and money from the wedding reception.

Looking back, it is horrifying to realize how naïve I was about pretty much everything, especially how to make a marriage and family work. Like all young people, I thought love, infatuation and sex could fix anything. I didn't realize a year and half of peace at the Binghams wasn't nearly enough time to undo a lifetime of abuse.

There were more than the usual newlywed bumps along the way for Rob and me. The first hurdle came within months after our wedding. I had been worried since our wedding day and my anxiety just got worse with each passing week. It seemed so obvious to me, but Rob had no idea I was feeling anything other than newly-wedded bliss.

One night I couldn't stand it any longer. My love for him was greater than my fear and I didn't want him to suffer needlessly anymore. "I understand if you are done with me," I blurted out. "I don't blame you. You deserve to be happy and I want you to spend your life with someone worthy of your love."

Rob was silent, lying in the dark next to me. After a long pause he asked quietly, "What are talking about?"

I sat up and replied, "You know, how I act. I know you are done with me and don't want me around. I am sorry I hurt you but I didn't want to lose you and now you know the truth about me."

Rob was quiet again, pondering. I steamrolled ahead, on a fast track to unburden my soul and set him free. "I know I'm not kind and I have done things in my life that you don't know about. I should have told you the truth, but I was afraid you wouldn't love me if you knew the 'real' Heather. Virginia told me all the time growing up that everyone outside the house was fooled. They all liked me, but if they knew the real me, they wouldn't. So I understand. It's not your fault. You had no way of knowing. If you want me to leave, I don't blame you."

I held my breath, waiting for the fateful blow that would end my only chance at happiness. But it didn't come. Instead, Rob sat up and put his arms around me. He held me and said, "I'm so sorry your mother said those things to you. She had no right. You are a wonderful person and there is no fake or real Heather. Just you. You are beautiful and smart and I love you. I'm not going anywhere and neither are you."

Once again, unconditional love helped me peel a layer of my old life off like caked-on dirt scrubbed off with fresh water.

In the spring of 1988 we were living on campus in married student housing. I was five months pregnant with our first child. We hadn't set out to get pregnant so soon into our marriage but as the joke goes, we were too poor to go out on a date so we stayed home and made a baby instead. It seemed like a highly entertaining, cost-saving idea at the time.

One afternoon I went to run errands and when I came back to our apartment, the neighbor downstairs stopped me. "Hey, your mom stopped by to see you a while ago. She was knocking on doors looking for you."

"My mom was here?" I asked, not comprehending the question as I asked it.

I was thinking "What mom? I don't have a mom. Maybe it was Mom Bingham, but that doesn't make sense. She knows where I live and why would she drive three hours from Phoenix to see me?"

My thoughts were interrupted by my neighbor. "Yeah, she said her name is Claudia, and she is coming to live with you. She had a big, black trash bag in a cart she was pulling. I think she was trying to move in."

I was stunned. Claudia? I hadn't seen her since I was seven years-old, the last time I spent a weekend with her and Ralph before we were taken to the Spencers. Claudia wasn't at home the day I met Ralph during my high school graduation trip. What is she doing here? How did she find me? My thoughts were firing a mile a minute.

"Is she here now?" I asked the neighbor, knowing full well everyone in the complex was going to know about this by nightfall.

"Nah, she left after I told her you were gone and probably wouldn't be back until this evening. She said she would come back tonight."

It was after three p.m. Rob would be at the Walgreen's distribution warehouse, where he worked from 3 p.m. to midnight. I called and he answered the phone, breathless. "What's going on? Are you alright?" he asked, concerned.

"Well, other than my life is falling apart, I'm fine." I then told him of my encounter with the neighbor.

When I was finished Rob asked, "So, what do you want to do?"

I wailed, "I don't know! I don't want to see her, I know

that."

"Are you sure? She is your mother, after all," he pointed out.

I tensed up, sensing he didn't get it. "I haven't seen her in years and I don't know what to expect. She is schizophrenic, for heaven's sake, and I definitely don't want her to know I'm pregnant. We don't know why she is here or what she is capable of."

Rob sighed and asked, "Do you want me to come home?"

"Yes. Please hurry," I said.

When he arrived home 20 minutes later, I was already pacing a hole in the living room rug. We talked and I stayed firm on not wanting to see Claudia. We agreed I would go to a friend's house across town. Rob would meet with Claudia, see what she wanted, and then call me. I left the apartment feeling grateful Rob was in my life and guilty because he was going to face what I was too weak to deal with. At 11 p.m., long past my nerves being shot, Rob showed up at the house I was waiting in. I peppered him with questions at the door. "What happened? What took so long? Is she still here?"

"Its ok, she's gone. I put her on the train back to Portland. Let's go home. I am beat." he said, scooping my jacket up off the couch.

On the way home he finished telling me the story. "She had a fight with Ralph and decided to leave him. She knew you got married when you sent a wedding invitation to Rex. She called the Spencers to get your address and phone number. They gave it to her and she got on a train to come here, planning to live with us. She had all her stuff in a black trash bag and had her mind made up. I told her she couldn't stay with us and she didn't like that at all. She insisted on seeing you. I told her, "No, that's not possible. She doesn't want to see you."

I cringed when he said that, thinking it made me sound just awful. Rob continued, "After that, I asked her if she had any money for a hotel room or a ticket back to Portland. She said no, she bought a one way ticket because she was going to live with us. She said she had a friend at the local Jehovah's Witness hall so I drove her over there."

Rob rubbed his eyes with exhaustion.

"No one was at the building but I got the phone number of the Overseer from the phone book. When I called the guy he said he knew Claudia from a phone call she made to them a few days ago asking if this was the closest Hall to the university and that she would need a place to stay when she came in town, just for one night. She spent last night with him and his family. I told him the situation and asked if he could help. He didn't want to, saying that his church wasn't set up for this kind of thing and that if we don't want her to stay, we should send her back. I asked if he could just take her for the night and put her on the train in the morning. We argued for a while because he didn't want her to stay another night, he didn't want to buy her a ticket back, and he didn't want to get any more involved in this situation. Finally Claudia called her Jehovah's Witness Overseer in Portland. He confirmed her membership to the Overseer here and agreed to send money to pay for her return ticket. I left her with the local Overseer, figuring they could handle her better than we could."

He looked completely spent but I just had to ask.

"How did she look?" He dropped his shoes on our bedroom floor.

"What? What do you mean?" he asked, confused.

"Claudia. You know, was she fat or skinny, was her hair long or short, were her clothes clean or dirty."

I knew full well how shallow I sounded but I was unable to stop myself.

He looked up at me from the end of the bed where he was sitting and said, "She looked ok. A lot like you actually but heavier. I don't know about her hair. She had a hat on the whole time."

He walked to his side of the bed and pulled the covers back. "I hate to do this, but I am exhausted. Dealing with your mother and the Jehovah's Witness guy just took it completely out of me."

After Claudia's visit I got curious. Over the years I had questions about her mental condition of schizophrenia. I found bits and pieces of information in encyclopedias and other reference books. I had been too afraid of the topic to check a book out from the library, but if a stray bit of information came my way, I paid attention.

One day on the television there was a public service commercial advertising a government office you could write to request pamphlets about a wide variety of subjects. One of the topics mentioned was mental illness. I decided it was time to find out the truth. I wrote a letter requesting information about schizophrenia, enclosing a dollar for postage and shipping. Within two weeks I received a package from Pueblo, Colorado with a fat pamphlet entitled, "Understanding Schizophrenia: A Family Guide." The first page started out, "If you are reading this, you are looking for information that is often times hard to find and understand." That was the understatement of the year.

It went on to explain the definition of schizophrenia, the known causes of it, the genetic links to it and the standard treatments for it. It was pretty bleak reading, especially the descriptions regarding paranoid schizophrenia, the kind Claudia had. I became frightened when I read the chances of me getting it were greatest in my 20s, tapering off until my 40s. In my 20s! I was 21 and pregnant with my first child. I spent the rest of the day despondent. I brooded, thinking about how Claudia must have felt as she had my brother and me taken away from her.

What would I do if I woke up with schizophrenia? Who would take care of my baby? Who would take care of me? Surely I couldn't expect Rob to deal with a schizophrenic wife the rest of his life. That wouldn't be fair. But what would he do with me? Would he put me in an institution, where I would be locked up the rest of my life? Would he raise our child with a new wife? I couldn't blame him, although it seemed too terrible a thought to consider.

By the time Rob got home I was in a tizzy of tears and despair. I was acting like I had been diagnosed with schizophrenia already and Rob had decisions to make. "What will you do with me? Where will you take me? How long will you wait to divorce me? Will you tell the baby about me, or just pretend it belongs to your new wife?"

My questions hit him hard and fast. It took him a while to calm me down and figure out what in the world I was talking about.

Rob's response to all my questions was, "I don't know what we would do if you got schizophrenia. I don't think you will get it. But I won't leave you and no one is taking away your child. We are a family and we will stay that way."

I chose to believe his reassurances.

Before I went to sleep that night, I said a long prayer of gratitude to Heavenly Father for sending Rob into my life.

11. THE PLOT THICKENS

While I was busy trying to make my own life, my brother was also creating a future for himself. Rex split his time between living with Ralph and Claudia, and Claudia's mother, Lennis. He finished high school, receiving a 'Certificate of Completion' when he was 20 years-old. He was able to stay in school longer than a typical student because he received special educational support, which by law requires students with special needs to be able to attend school until 21 years-old. Rex flunked every English and Math class he took in high school until he was put into a modified class his last year. At graduation Rex read on a fourth grade level. He had trouble doing math beyond addition and subtraction and relied on keeping his life simple due to an inability to process multi-step tasks.

After Rex got his high school Certificate of Completion he joined the Army. Claudia was furious, she was opposed to military service. Ralph signed his parental consent without telling her. Her anger didn't last long, Rex was discharged two months and twenty-eight day later for having flat feet. Rex was upset he couldn't stay in. He made a couple of friends in the Army and discovered he had a passion for computers.

Once out of the Army he went back to Ralph and Claudia. Ralph's career as a dishwasher ended when the cafeteria he worked at for 22 years was torn down. Ralph and Rex began delivering newspapers. That job imploded the day someone drove into Ralph and Rex while they were loading newspapers into the trunk of their car at the newspaper office. Both Ralph and Rex suffered back and leg injuries. The driver's insurance company gave them money for their injuries and Ralph's totaled car.

When our first child was a few months old I had a surprising phone call. "Haddie, this is your mom, Claudia. We are coming to see you tomorrow. What time will you and your husband be home?"

My mind raced. Claudia? Ralph? Here? Tomorrow? Now? Do I want this? What will Rob say? How can I get out of this?

"Um...I'm not sure when we will be available tomorrow. I will have to talk to my husband and see. Where are you?" I asked, hoping they were still in Portland but knowing better.

"We are on our way to your house. We have Rex with us and he is going to live with the Spencers. We will be to your place about one o'clock tomorrow. I'll call before we get there so you can be ready. Bye, Haddie."

The phone went dead.

When I told Rob about Claudia's call we decided I needed to be there. Not knowing how Claudia and Ralph would behave or what their intentions were, we decided to leave our daughter with a babysitter. The next day I received a phone call at noon from Claudia and I told them to meet us in a parking lot on campus.

Rob and I went to the parking lot and pulled our car alongside Ralph's station wagon. It was loaded down with all their possessions. It was obvious they were moving. They had received the insurance settlement from Ralph and Rex's accident and decided it was time for a change. They didn't know exactly where they were going but part of the trip was to take Rex back to the Spencers because he no longer wanted to live with Ralph and Claudia.

All three of them were dirty and stunk like they hadn't showered in days. Rex and Ralph's hair was overgrown, greasy and hung well below their ears. Standing side by side they looked remarkably alike. Rex was taller than I was and had some meat on his bones. He looked good. He had trouble keeping eye contact and kept interrupting Claudia and Ralph, trying to interject his thoughts into the conversation. Actually, all of them interrupted each other constantly so it wasn't long before Rob and I were just nodding our heads in agreement, not sure who to look at or whose conversation we were following. It didn't seem to matter; the three were so intent on getting their words out none of them was checking to see if it was being received or if anyone else was speaking. After visiting with us for a short time they decided to leave and I called the Spencers to let them know the Wades were coming. Virginia was not happy, as this visit was news to her. It didn't take long for me to get a call back from Virginia telling me Ralph and Claudia had arrived with bad cases of lice, were dirty and not making a lot of sense. They were openly talking about how much money they had received from the insurance settlement. Virginia was concerned they might get robbed if they talked to the wrong person.

After staying a day or two with the Spencers, Ralph and Claudia decided to head to Texas where they had some distant family. I was relieved I had chosen to meet them in the parking lot and had not taken them to our apartment. I didn't feel bad that Ralph and Claudia left the Spencer's house infested with lice. I took satisfaction thinking the Spencers got what they deserved. I was worried about Rex being back with the Spencers but I was even more anxious about what I was going to do with him when he got kicked out of their house again. I assumed it was just a matter of time before Rex would be back on my doorstep. I didn't think Rob would be very happy about it. I was dreading the thought of having to choose between my husband and my brother.

Within a few days the Spencers kicked Rex out again. In a surprising move, he didn't come to me. Instead, he went to live with Matthew, who was working full-time doing manual labor on a construction site. Matthew lived in a mobile home in the same trailer park as Virginia and Harley. They gave up their house soon after I moved out, due to the downward pull of lower middle-class living. Rex didn't get a job and was in his usual routine of not cleaning himself up, eating all the food and leaving dirty dishes around the trailer. Matthew was his long-suffering self and didn't make any demands on Rex.

The next year Rob and I moved with our daughter to Brigham Young University in Utah, where Rob transferred to get his degree in construction management. I continued with my education in public relations. I figured I would be good at it because I knew how to put a happy face on bad situations.

Within months of our move, the Spencers moved to Ogden, about two hours north of us. Matthew and Rex stayed behind in Arizona in the trailer park. I didn't know they had moved until I got a phone call from Virginia telling me that my little sisters/nieces, Madeline and McKenzie, now teenagers, were sent by the State of Arizona to live with them due to allegations of abuse against their father and stepmother.

Marcus denied he did anything wrong with his girls, but as Virginia described some of the alleged abuse, it sounded plausible to me. I knew he and his wife were very harsh with the girls when I was in high school. Now the girls were living unprotected with the people who created their dad. Virginia complained to me that the girls had lousy attitudes and kept asking to live in Mississippi with their mother, who they hadn't seen in years. I asked Virginia what she was doing to help the girls heal from the abuse they suffered. She said they were requiring the girls to stay in their bedroom and read the scriptures until they were able to forgive their father and stepmother. She and Harley told them they needed to forgive their dad for his sins and learn to love him.

When I heard that, a chill went down my spine. That was a tactic they used on Emelia, pulling her out of school in her freshman year and making her stay in her room for nine months, reading only scriptures to heal her rebelliousness. She solved her problem by getting pregnant and married in her sophomore year of high school. I didn't want the same fate for

Madeline and McKenzie. Nothing against Emelia's plan, but it was fraught with life complications I didn't want my little sisters to deal with. I wanted them to be safe and happy.

I offered to take the girls for a week to give Virginia and Harley a break. During their stay at our apartment the girls confirmed the abuse from their dad and stepmother. It was obvious they needed help. I felt like I was reliving the past all over again. I talked to a couple of social work majors in our housing complex about my options. They told me I had zero chance of getting the girls into my custody without a huge legal battle with the Spencers. It would cost money and take time, of which I had neither. The whole week was very upsetting to me and I felt even worse taking them back to the Spencers. I felt helpless, enraged and sick to my stomach. Once again, just like with Rex, I was unable to rescue someone I loved.

Just days after the girls' visit, I got a terrible headache. I went to an optometrist for glasses, a family doctor, the ER and a neurologist, all of whom gave me different medications. None of it helped my worsening headache. By the third week I was banging my head on the floor of our bedroom, delirious from pain. Rob called the neurologist again and he agreed to see me.

When the doctor took a look at me, he called a neurosurgeon. It was decided I needed emergency brain surgery. A ventricle that drained fluid off my brain had collapsed, building pressure in my skull. In infants it is diagnosed as hydrocephalus, a condition extremely rare to see in adults without any cause. I was in bad shape when the surgery was performed, out of my mind with pain and alternating between being unresponsive and talking gibberish.

Before the surgery Rob laid his hands on my head and he gave me a blessing of healing. He felt at peace and had a strong feeling of comfort. I have no memory of anything besides being in the doctor's office and him telling Rob I needed surgery immediately.

After surgery the surgeon told Rob to prepare himself because the fluid pressure was extremely high inside my skull, much worse than they expected. When they cut open my head the backed-up fluid came out with such force it flew across the operating room and hit the wall. In his opinion there was no way I could not have permanent brain damage from the delayed diagnosis. He recommended Rob call family and make arrangements to move closer to them. I was going to require long-term nursing care and he was going to need help caring for our 18 month-old baby and me.

I woke up with my head half-shaved, my bed surrounded by medical personnel all very interested in my well-being. For three days I had a non-stop parade of hospital people checking in on me, asking me questions. I thought they were super friendly people who were extremely interested in their patients. I finally told them I needed to stop talking, my throat was raw from the exertion of keeping up my end of the conversations. It took months for me to realize I was fascinating only because I was the current medical freak show. How self-centered was I to think strangers really cared about my favorite music, movies and books.

During the follow-up visit a few weeks later, the neurosurgeon was shocked at how well I had recovered. He said it was a miracle it was even caught in time. It is usually fatal, no one realizing there is a problem until it is too late. A nurse in the ER had died the week before I was admitted from the same condition. She had a terrible headache, went home from work early and went to bed. She didn't wake up. Rob asked if extreme emotional stress could be a possible cause of such a condition. The neurosurgeon replied without hesitation, "Absolutely. Entirely possible." On the way home from the doctor's office I had to decide once again to save my life and let the Spencers go. The stress of feeling helpless to rescue my little sisters had almost killed me. I wasn't emotionally strong enough to fight the Spencers to save my little sisters and I didn't have the money to hire lawyers to help. I said a prayer for the girls' safety and didn't call the Spencers to check on the well-being again. All I could do is pray my sisters had someone to rescue them, like I found Mr. Gross, Stephanie's family and the Binghams. I agonized it couldn't be me, but I couldn't die or be in a nursing home over it. I gave all I could.

While I was recovering from surgery, Emelia called to talk to me. She and her husband had followed the Spencers to Utah. They had four children and were very close to Harley and Virginia. Rob explained I had life-threatening brain surgery and had just gotten home from the hospital. Emelia told Virginia I had brain surgery and Virginia's comment was, "It couldn't have been that big of a deal or Heather would have called to tell us."

Emelia called Rob back and told him Virginia's reaction. I was hurt but not surprised. Why would they start acting like loving parents just because my head almost exploded? Rob couldn't believe their response. He had heard my stories about my childhood, but hadn't yet experienced them for himself. It was just another in a long list of examples of their not caring.

Even though I had made a miraculous recovery, I was terrified of complications. Rob and I were warned by the doctors that I shouldn't ever ride horses, snow ski, water ski, ice skate, parachute from airplanes or do anything that might cause a head injury. It could kill me. As soon as we could we moved to Colorado, where Rob's parents now lived. Rob transferred to Colorado State University to continue his education. Other than struggling with reading comprehension for a year and losing my magical ability to spell anything, I was physically fine. Emotionally, I was a hot mess of fear. Every time I got even the slightest twinge of a headache I panicked, thinking my shunt had failed and I was going to die. The neurosurgeon told us that on average a shunt lasts between 5-7 years before needing to be replaced and the only way to know if it had gone bad was to get another headache that gradually built up to excruciating pain. I hadn't considered the idea of needing repeated brain surgeries the rest of my life and was hyper-vigilant about any change in my body. I drove Rob crazy with my constant need of reassurance that the pupils of my eyes didn't look dilated, like they were when I needed surgery.

During the years we were in school, Rob worked full-time

as a night janitor and attended class full-time during the day. During our 18 months at BYU in Utah the only job Rob could find was on a local farm, milking cows. He learned all about managing a dairy herd while juggling his classes, our toddler Jennifer and my head. My brain surgery incident required him to change schools and in the process he lost credits that wouldn't transfer.

After eight years and two more cheap entertainment offspring, Rob graduated with his Bachelor's degree. I marveled at the dedication he showed to getting his college education. I felt proud and also guilty for putting him through what he feared the most before we got married. It was almost like he knew ahead of time that by asking me to marry him, he was volunteering to go down a very, very difficult path. And at that point, it hadn't even begun to get hard.

12. ANOTHER CHANCE TO DO IT RIGHT

Matthew's patience with Rex finally ran out. He put Rex on a bus sending him back to the Spencers in Utah. When he arrived at Harley and Virginia's house, they refused him. Rex decided this was his opportunity to fulfill his dream of living off the land. He bought camping supplies with the last of his insurance settlement money and hiked into the mountains surrounding Ogden, Utah. He pitched his tent, preparing to live the rest of his life in the wilderness as a mountain man. After a few days, Rex realized he needed to tweak his plan. He left his campsite and headed back in to town to get more supplies. While in town his seemingly abandoned camp site was discovered by some hikers who grew concerned and called authorities.

In Rex's personal belongings the deputies found information leading back to the Spencers. When questioned Virginia told them she had no idea why he was in the mountains. A search party was quickly formed based on the general description provided by Harley and Virginia. While standing with reporters, preparing to go on the evening news to talk about the mysterious disappearance of her son, Virginia saw Rex walking through the search headquarters. He had joined the search teams to help find the poor man lost in the mountains. She was very embarrassed when Rex, in all innocence, protested he had no idea everyone was looking for him. The search was cancelled as quickly as it was organized.

Rex was taken to the homeless shelter in Salt Lake City, where he was given a job and housing through the Mormon church's Deseret Industries, a program designed to help people in need. He worked sorting donated shoes, a job he hated and that completely stressed him out. He wanted to work on computers, not match piles of shoes to their mates. After a few months of sharing an apartment, Rex's assigned roommate split, leaving him to pay all the bills which of course he couldn't. He shortly thereafter quit DI and was evicted from his apartment.

Homeless once again, Rex decided it was time to get to the core issue, to solve the real problem. The problem wasn't in him or in his learning disabilities. It was in the federal tax codes and how wealth was distributed in America. While working at DI he started studying politics and tax codes in his spare time. Now that he was freed from the responsibilities of paying rent and utilities, he focused his attention where it was needed. He decided to go to Washington D.C. to meet with the legislature and make his case for tax reform.

The reality that Rex had no money or transportation was only a minor bump in the road. He packed his sleeping bag and backpack and set out to walk across America. He was picked up a couple of times and was given rides for short periods, but most of the time he walked. After three days of walking and sleeping at night along highway 80 heading east thru Wyoming, Rex became utterly exhausted. He was hungry, cold and angry. As he lay in his sleeping bag a few feet off the highway he began addressing God aloud, saying, "Why have you done this to me? I am so alone. No one cares about me. I have no family. I have no friends. I don't know why I am not good enough to be loved. I want to know if you are really there and care about me or I just want to die. I don't want to be alone anymore."

He began sobbing, feeling the depths of isolation and rejection. After a few minutes in acute suffering, he experienced a sensation of incredible calm, like a waterfall of cascading peace. He later told me, "After I prayed to Heavenly Father, his Son, Jesus Christ came to me and told me He loved me and that I would never be alone again. I felt so warm and happy I knew it was really real. And I knew beyond a shadow of a doubt that Jesus loved me and that He was my best friend and would never leave me."

The next morning Rex was picked up by a trucker on highway 80 and given a ride into Cheyenne, Wyoming. He decided to stay in Cheyenne because his new Best Friend, Jesus, told him he was needed there and he had an important work to do. Rex's plan to go to Washington, D.C. was temporarily put on hold as he followed the direction of his new Best Friend.

Upon walking into town, he was pointed to the local homeless shelter. A social worker there helped him finish his application for Social Security Disability Income, a process he started in Utah but hadn't finished. He was evaluated and granted benefits based on chronic back and neck pain from the car accident, learning difficulties and mental health problems. He was also assigned a state case manager who was to help him live independently.

Rex worked part-time at Burger King and found it difficult. His teenage co-workers delighted in giving him a hard time, seeing how far they could push him until he lost his temper. After a few months he was let go because he couldn't keep up the pace.

Rex didn't know how to drive and relied on public transportation, riding a bike and walking to get around. His case manager arranged his apartment in Cheyenne. It was a run-down studio on the bad side of town. It didn't take long for him to invite a stranger he met on the streets to live with him. Unfortunately, Rex's new roommate brought drugs and pornography into the apartment. Within a matter of days all the occupants of the surrounding apartments were Rex's 'friends' because he had a telephone. The drug users and prostitutes in the neighborhood used his phone to make their connections while Rex was giddy with joy at finally being needed.

He attended the local Mormon church congregation on Sundays but was ostracized because of his dirty clothes, stinky body and his habit of gravitating toward the young children. Frankly, he scared adults and no one wanted anything to do with him. I was contacted by the church headquarters in Salt Lake City. They told me Rex was in Cheyenne, Wyoming and that he requested I call him. I was confused as to how he ended up in Wyoming. The last I knew he was living in Utah. No one in the Spencer family told me had moved. I called Rex's phone number and we had a disjointed conversation as I tried to connect the dots between when he lived in Utah and how he ended up living in Cheyenne. He wasn't able to say much beyond his Best Friend told him to stay put.

We were living in Windsor, Colorado, an hour south of Rex. Rob and I began visiting him regularly and we were alarmed by the people who had access to his apartment. We talked to him about kicking out his roommate and he couldn't understand our concerns. All he cared about is that was his roommate needed his help. He was doing Jesus' work. Rob and I finally intervened while Rex was out running errands one day. We told his roommate to move on and helped him pack. Rex grieved that loss for weeks. I felt terrible, understanding how desperately Rex wanted to be needed but the fact was, it was a dangerous situation.

At the same time we were trying to clean out the local riffraff from his place, Rex started complaining about having headaches. On one of our visits, when Rob and I opened the door of his apartment, the smell of gas was overwhelming. I called the utility company and they came out right away. They determined there was a gas leak in his apartment and shut off the utilities while they repaired it. Rex called his social worker and temporary housing was arranged. It turned out to be the break we were looking for. Since his apartment was officially declared unlivable with no heat or hot water, another apartment was made available across town.

He moved into a clean, safe apartment in a high-rise

building called Shoshoni Manor. Most of the building occupants were elderly people living on fixed incomes. Rex was the youngest person living there and he was viewed with suspicion by the other residents. The building had one main entrance that required a security code. Rex's apartment was on the 4th floor. Rex's old neighborhood friends tried to gain access to his apartment but were turned away at the door. For the first time in his life, Rex was physically safe and had his personal needs met. The money he received from Social Security Disability and the subsidized housing meant he had food, shelter and stability.

I was anxious to introduce Rex to my family and to make up for our thirteen years apart.

13. NEARER TO GOD

With Rex's move into a new apartment came a new congregation at a different Mormon church building and another chance to make friends. His first Sunday in Shoshoni Manor, Rex excitedly went to church. He showed up, unkempt and stinky as ever. The bishop, Thelton Skipper, was alerted to his presence by a concerned adult. Rex was in the foyer telling children he was Santa Claus and was going to bring them all presents. Bishop Skipper invited Rex into his office to talk.

In The Church Of Jesus Christ of Latter-Day Saints, the bishop is considered the leader of the congregation and is assisted by two other men as counselors to make sure all church member's needs are met. It requires on average 30-35 hours a week to perform the duties of a bishop. This responsibility is carried out as all local church positions, without pay. It is also required that the bishop be married and have a job to support his family. It is not a church calling for the faint of heart.

The bishop confirmed Rex was an active member of the church and had no history of violent behavior. As bishop Skipper talked, Rex produced a computer-generated application for incorporation of Santa Claus, Inc. This was Rex's proof that he was legally able to work as Santa Claus. Bishop Skipper calmly told Rex that even though he had official paperwork, it didn't make him Santa Claus and he could not tell the children he was Santa. Rex agreed that until he could formally become Santa he wouldn't bother anyone with that. He stayed for Sacrament Meeting and then left. The next Sunday Rex showed up again and met with the bishop. He brought with him a computer-generated Last Will and Testament leaving all of his belongings to the church. The fact he had no possessions of value didn't bother him. This started a pattern of every Sunday Rex presenting to Bishop Skipper a new business idea, non-profit company idea or some scheme to earn money. Each time the bishop would patiently listen and point out why the idea wouldn't work. Rex seemed to trust the bishop's opinion and didn't argue with him.

Bishop Skipper spent his share of time counseling with Rex making sure he had food, clothes and a purpose at church. The bishop intuitively understood that Rex needed to have a way to serve and show love to others.

One day Bishop Skipper asked Rex about his family. Rex talked about our foster family, our adopted family and the abuse he suffered. He told him he was beaten with belts, boat paddles and sticks. He explained he was banished to his room and starved for years. Rex even explained the one thing he hadn't been able to overcome, his need to be Santa Claus. While living with the Spencers, Rex only celebrated one Christmas. After that, he wasn't allowed to participate in Christmas because Harley and Virginia said he wasn't worthy of it. He was sent to his room while the rest of the family gathered around the Christmas tree on Christmas Eve. Virginia read the story of Jesus' birth from the Bible, and we opened presents. He got none. He didn't get to celebrate his birthday or any other holiday, so why would he be worthy of Christmas?

Bishop Skipper told me Rex didn't show any emotion while he talked; he was very matter-of-fact. Bishop Skipper did the crying as he listened. He begged Rex to tell him the names of our adoptive parents so he could notify church authorities of the abuse but Rex refused. He didn't want the pain of reliving it again and just wanted to put it in the past. Bishop Thelton Skipper is the only person to whom Rex ever told the horrors of his childhood. The gift that Bishop Skipper gave Rex was the same unconditional love others gave me. It was clear to the bishop that although Rex had cognitive weaknesses, he was not a threat to anyone. Because of Bishop Skipper's acceptance of Rex, the rest of the congregation followed his lead and came to think of Rex as just a quirky member of their church family.

John Carmen, who was a counselor to the bishop, took Rex shopping for new clothes and stressed the importance of personal cleanliness. Rex showed up at church wearing his new clothes looking great except he refused to wear his new dress shoes. He said he didn't like them. He didn't tell them he had horribly flat feet and that the stiff dress shoes were too painful to wear. He just told them that his tennis shoes were easier to walk in to and from church. Rex was assigned to be the greeter at church. He stood at the entrance to the chapel, handing out programs for Sunday service and shaking hands. Rex took his job very seriously. He couldn't sit still during the sacrament meeting and changed seats at least three or four times during the meeting, covering all areas of the chapel. Each adult was given a program and everyone was given a welcoming handshake, even if it took the whole meeting to get the job done. I'm convinced there has never been a more through greeter in all of the 180+ years of the Mormon church.

Rex fully participated during adult Sunday school class, often to the consternation of the teacher. He answered every question and didn't give anyone else a chance to contribute. He could only read and write on a 4th grade level yet he had a deep understanding of the scriptures, sometimes knowing more about a scriptural passage than anyone else in the room. Bishop Skipper once asked Rex how he knew so much gospel doctrine, thinking how Rex struggled to remember to brush his teeth half the time. Rex replied that Jesus, his Best Friend, taught him.

Bishop Skipper thought of Rex's disabilities as if Rex was really, really smart but he just had one wire in his brain that sometimes disconnected. Some days Rex was very good and understood perfectly. Other days his thinking wasn't quite right and he wouldn't make a lot of sense.

After a year or two Thelton Skipper was released as bishop of the ward and he was made the Stake President, presiding over several congregations in the Cheyenne, Wyoming area. His counselor, John Carmen was made the new bishop of the congregation. This reshuffling of leadership assured Rex's relationships with his spiritual leaders continued uninterrupted.

John Carmen was a family physician in Cheyenne and he became not only Rex's Bishop, but also his medical doctor. Rex considered him to be his exclusive physician and walked into his clinic, breezing past the office staff, going directly to Dr. Carmen's personal desk. It created such havoc with the staff that Dr. Carmen was forced to tell Rex if he needed something he was not allowed to go to the office. He should just leave a message and the doctor would make a house call to check on Rex before he went home. I laughed because Rex was right, he did have an exclusive physician. No one else, not even the most beloved patients got home visits from a physician anymore.

As President Skipper and Bishop Carmen treated Rex with love and respect, always being straight forward and direct in their approach with him, Rex blossomed. Bishop Carmen kept an electric shaver in his desk at church for Rex to use if he forgot to shave. Rex responded to their efforts by showing up at church looking clean and appropriate without needing to be reminded.

Rex arrived early to church every Sunday to set out chairs and do whatever the Bishop asked that day. He was given the added assignment of preparing the church program for Sundays. He treated this task like a paid job. Rex purchased a computer from a local company on an installment plan and made monthly payments from his disability check. He only accepted information for the program through his e-mail. As this was years before most people had e-mail, it was a source of frustration to those who needed notices put in the bulletin. Rex refused to add their information to the program if they told him face-to-face, called him on the phone or even if they wrote it all out for him. It had to be sent through e-mail. He was trying to do his best to drag the congregation into the computer age. Rex insisted e-mail was the proper way to communicate information. Anything else was unprofessional.

I was so grateful Rex had church leaders who finally understood him. I was thrilled he had a case manager and a safe place to live. It was nothing short of a miracle and I was glad Rex's Best Friend told him to stay in Cheyenne. It was exactly where he needed to be.

14. REX'S BEST FRIEND

The state case worker assigned to Rex called me, frustrated because Rex was stubborn and refused to take advice. The case manager said Rex had a severe case of defensiveness and acted like other people's ideas were meaningless. He explained to me this was a common defense tactic for people who had learned not to trust others. Unfortunately it made it impossible for him to guide Rex to do something he didn't want to do. The case manager had met with his team leaders repeatedly trying to figure out how to break down the wall of mistrust. He reached out to me in a moment of desperation, looking for any insight I could give to help him in his duties.

I listened to the case manager and was touched by his dedication to his job. I didn't expect anyone from a government agency to care about my brother on such a deep level. I knew the statistics, that all social service agencies struggled with hundreds and thousands of 'Rex's' every day. I decided to trust him and asked if Rex ever told him his story. I could hear him flipping through papers and he said he had no record of my brother prior to him showing up at the homeless shelter in downtown Cheyenne.

"Well, do you have time to listen?" I asked, not wanting to go down this path unless I could thoroughly explain it.

"Sure," he replied. "I have plenty of time right now."

"Well, get ready to take notes because I have a story for you."

For the first time ever, I told my brother's complete history to someone. When I was finished, I detected a shift in the case manager's tone.

"Wow. I had no idea Rex had been through all that. That is the worst case of child abuse I have ever heard of," he said.

"Really?" I asked, knowing only of horrific child abuse cases I read about in the newspapers. "Well, the worst case that a child survived," he amended himself.

I told him the only people who had the ability to get Rex's attention were the bishop and stake president at church because they treated Rex with respect and love. I explained I won Rex's cooperation because I always brought food, so the case manager needed to pick his tool.

"Are you going to start baking pies for Rex or are you going to do something else?" I teased the case manager.

"Uh, I guess I need to ask my wife to give me dessert lessons," he joked.

The next time I ran into the case manager at Rex's apartment the change was apparent. Rex was relaxed and the men sat at the kitchen table, talking easily. I didn't see any evidence of a pie on the table so I assumed they found their own way to communicate and it was obviously working. That was the last call about problems I received from anyone working with Rex.

Rex lived in the Shoshoni high rise apartment near the mall for five years. Over those five years, our family traditions became set. He lived in a building with mainly elderly people and we had three young children. Rex got so excited at our coming to visit that he was loud and hyper. This in turn got the children loud and hyper. They fed off each other's energy.

Soon enough the jumping and joyful whooping and hollering was a problem for the neighbors. In desperation, we started a unique family tradition.

For Thanksgiving and Christmas, we drove up early and brought the full holiday meal to eat at Rex's apartment. It was a holiday brunch instead of dinner. We ate and were finished before many of Rex's neighbors even put their turkeys in the oven. Before anyone got too wound up, we loaded everyone in the car and went to the early matinee movies and watched a family show.

Movie theatres are one of the few places open on a holiday that is warm and safe for kids to get a little rowdy. Since we went to the 11 a.m. showing, there were very few people besides us and the employees running the theater. Once we got lucky and we were the only customers in the whole building.

We stretched out like royalty and I let Rex and the kids play hide-and-seek in the darkened theater while Rob and I relaxed, thoroughly enjoying the live-action Disney film "101 Dalmatians."

By the time the film ended, Rex and the kids were spent and ready to take a nap. We dropped Rex off at his apartment. He was anxious to dig into the leftovers we put in his fridge. The hour-long drive back to Colorado was blessedly silent as the children snoozed in the backseat and Rob and I congratulated ourselves on the most stress-free holiday ever.

The rest of the year we made it a point to take Rex and the kids to the park. Rex loved playing on the playground, pushing the kids on swings and going down the slides with them. We had to keep an eye on Rex as much as our children because his habit of wanting to play with all the little children created concern among other parents.

It is so hard to be an eight year-old boy in a grown man's body. Rex's case manager told us he was banished from the Cheyenne Public Library because he'd make a beeline to the children's section and try to strike up a conversation with the children. It never became any easier, knowing the other parents thought he was a pedophile. I didn't blame anyone for being concerned. How could anyone know from looking at him that Rex was still just a kid inside?

Rex's obsession with the idea of being Santa Claus never

waned. The years of cruelty spent with the Spencers made a deep impression on him. He constantly tried to earn money to buy Christmas toys for all the children of the world. It was a year-round project for him that became frenzied in the months before Christmas. No one understood why it was so important to him for every child to have toys for Christmas. It stabbed my heart each time I was aware of his schemes to earn money for the 'Santa Claus' project. I felt constantly reminded that I had failed Rex in our childhood. I didn't protect him like I should have and I could see right in front of me the results of my weakness.

Many times he started home-based businesses selling jewelry, knick-knacks or whatever the latest 'Get Rich Quick Scheme' was. Rex did eventually save enough money to pay the filing fees to legally incorporate "Santa Claus, Inc." in the state of Wyoming. The Bishop talked to him every November, giving him the annual reminder that it wasn't appropriate to tell parents and children he would make sure they had toys for Christmas. That would be butting into the parent's responsibility to be Santa for their children. What Rex couldn't explain was he knew that even if you had a family, it didn't mean you would get Christmas.

As time went on, the issues of personal cleanliness and keeping his apartment reasonably clean resolved themselves. Several times the Relief Society organization of women from his congregation went to his apartment to help him clean up. Other members who were assigned to keep an eye on Rex also helped out when needed. Rex learned to keep himself and his apartment clean. I learned to not bring dishes and extra stuff for his apartment. It was too hard for him to keep organized if he had more than a couple of plates, a few cups and a few pieces of silverware. The simpler, the better. All I could do to show my love for him was offer my time and attention.

Rex was very passionate about computers. The gift of his military experience was the opportunity to fall in love with computers. Rex couldn't drive, couldn't keep a job, couldn't break through the wall of social rules, but he understood computers.

His case manager sent him to the Association for Retarded Citizens (ARC) center in Cheyenne, thinking they could help him occupy his restless mind and give him something to do besides bother his neighbors or hang out with his shady 'friends' on the streets. When Rex went to the nearby ARC office he walked in and introduced himself.

He didn't have anyone with him, he didn't look like a possible client needing services and he didn't tell them he needed help. Instead, he noticed the secretary was having problems with her computer and he offered to help. She gratefully accepted his offer. When he fixed the software problem he offered to volunteer in the office, working with the computers. No one noticed his social delays because compared to the people with more severe disabilities, Rex was fine. When Rex's case manager called the ARC to see how he was doing, they were confused. Imagine their surprise to discover the guy volunteering in the office and fixing their computers was supposed to be receiving services from them.

Rex went into every situation with the attitude, "How can I help?" He had a firm conviction that his Best Friend sent him to help the people of Cheyenne, Wyoming. He never stopped looking for opportunities to fulfill his mission.

Rex liked to bear his testimony at church on Fast and Testimony Sundays, which are held church-wide on the first Sunday of every month. It is an opportunity for anyone in the congregation to publicly speak about their spiritual experiences and to testify of Christ. It is basically a monthly 'open mic' at the pulpit, for good or bad. Rex never missed an opportunity to bear his testimony and would make a point of talking about his Best Friend, Jesus and how his Best Friend loved everyone. Most people in church took his comments with a grain of salt, not disparaging his heartfelt testimony, but also not encouraging any possible nuttiness.

One Sunday he walked to church (at least a mile) participated in the meetings, walked home, got an apple and then returned to the meetinghouse because he noticed the bishop was having a very long day in meetings and thought he might like something to eat. Rex loved Bishop Carmen and trusted him as fully as President Skipper.

Rex was sent a credit card in the mail with a pre-approved $200 spending limit. Rex thought that was great. He spent the money extended in credit and then was greatly confused and panicked when the bills started showing up, demanding payment. Rex lived on Social Security Disability payments and had no way to pay the credit card bill. He went to Bishop Carmen for advice on what to do. The bishop told him not to worry about it. The fact it would stay on his credit score as an unpaid debt was a good incentive for future card companies not to be so foolish with their lines of credit. The whole thing mystified Rex. "Why did they give me money to spend if they knew I couldn't pay it back?" he asked Bishop Carmen.

"I don't know Rex, but hopefully they have learned their lesson," the bishop replied. Rex shrugged and said, "I'm glad I could help them." Even a credit card bill was an opportunity for him to serve.

15. BAD GUYS AND BAD NEWS

Unfortunately Rex had plenty of experience with people who took advantage of his trusting nature. With his Social Security check he needed to pay for his day-to-day expenses but there were so many temptations for him. His friends at the pawn shops and secondhand stores reserved things just for him, like video games, toys, anything a young boy would like and Rex hated to disappoint his friends.

I got a call from him not long after he moved into the high-rise apartment, his voice in a panic. "I have to go to court. They want to kick me out of my apartment. Would you come and pay the bill so I can stay?"

I had no idea what he was talking about. "I have to be at court on Wednesday so they won't kick me out," he said, his voice rising with each word.

It turned out he hadn't paid his rent for several months and was on the verge of being evicted. He had spent his money on fun stuff. At that point I hadn't yet gotten involved deeply in his finances, knowing he had a case manager. What I didn't know is that a case manager doesn't automatically take over someone's finances. He was there to make sure Rex was safe, not being harmful to himself or others, and not to micromanage his personal choices. I went to the courthouse the next day to discover my brother was subject to an official eviction hearing. Thank goodness public housing has due process. Rex would have never told me about his money problems if he hadn't been summoned to court. He didn't want the Bishop to know of his predicament, fearing he would get into trouble. Appearing before a judge really scared him. The public housing officer stated Rex hadn't paid his $89 monthly rent for three months and must leave. I sat with Rex at the defendant's table and was asked by the judge to introduce myself. I did, then explained I had no idea Rex's rent hadn't been paid and that if he were kicked out, he would have nowhere to go. Rex sat meekly silent, his head bowed in contriteness. The judge asked if I would make sure from then on that Rex's rent was paid. I eagerly agreed, realizing it would seriously complicate my life if Rex ended up with no home. I couldn't fathom how difficult it would be to talk Rob into letting Rex live with us. It just wasn't an option.

The judge said Rex wouldn't be evicted this time but if he ever did this again, he would be out. The housing officer protested but the judge told him to be quiet.

I was joyous and so relieved. Rex had such a good thing going in Cheyenne and I was sick at the thought of what would happen to him (and me) without his apartment. My top priority now was to make sure Rex kept his home. I dreaded the thought of ever having to ask Rob if my brother could live with us.

That day Rex and I contacted his case manager. He was speechless when I explained what had just happened in court. The three of us arranged for the case manager to receive Rex's Social Security money, pay his bills for him and give him the remaining funds, which averaged $35 a month. When Rex realized he couldn't spend his money like he used to, he complained but I was content knowing his needs were met. The case manager pointed out to Rex that if he wanted more money he could forego paying tithing to the church and keep that 10% for himself. Rex argued that point. He was passionate that tithes belonged to his Best Friend so that others could be helped. Rex didn't mind paying tithing at all. He minded paying for soap and taxes.

Before the case manager controlled Rex's finances,

someone stole his checkbook. They wrote bad checks forging his signature all over town. Rex got notices from his bank that his account was overdrawn, and then he got phone calls and letters from collection agencies trying to settle the bad checks. He was really upset about it and couldn't understand how he owed $190 for basketball shoes he never bought and big dinners at fancy restaurants where he hadn't eaten. At first no one at the collection agencies would talk to me because I didn't have Power of Attorney over Rex's finances. A clerk at one of the collection agencies told me I needed to show proof of my claim that Rex didn't write the checks. I filed a report at the police station, showing them copies of the bad checks provided by the bank. The signatures on the checks obviously didn't match Rex's handwriting. They gave me a copy of the criminal complaint, and I took that to the collection agencies. As we made the rounds to the collection agencies they were rude in their dealings with Rex, even with me standing next to him, explaining the situation. I was shocked at the intimidation tactics they used to scare him. In one office, a clerk apologized for the shoddy treatment Rex received. As I left the building, her apology rang in my ears and I thought, "You won't last another month. You have too good a heart to keep doing this mean-spirited job."

Although Cheyenne, Wyoming was where Jesus told Rex he was needed, it was not a paradise for him. Bad people live everywhere. Rex became acquainted with a special kind of evil on July 8, 1995. It was a hot, stuffy summer day, cooling down only late at night. He went for a walk at 1:30 a.m., something he did quite often during the summer months. He wandered over towards Mylar Park to see if anyone was around to play with. Two thugs that Rex didn't recognize but who knew him to be 'slow' and friendly, offered him a ride to the park. He happily accepted, thinking they would all play on the swing sets together. When he was in the car they asked if he had any money. Of course, he didn't. When they got to the Mylar Park parking lot the thugs took a concrete lawn statue they had previously stolen and proceeded to beat Rex with it until he was unconscious. They left him to die in the parking lot. He was discovered by another passerby a few hours later.

Rex was in intensive care for three days. He had a severe concussion and the right side of his skull and face were badly broken.

Back in Colorado, Rob and I had no idea there was even a problem. I typically called Rex every couple of weeks and we scheduled a trip to Cheyenne at least every six weeks, depending on if any of our kids were sick or had other things going on. I fully relied on Rex's case manager and the people at church to keep an eye on him. My own family was all-consuming and I was glad to not have to worry about Rex's day-to-day needs.

It was only when Rex miraculously was able to talk and gave his name and information to the hospital that Bishop Carmen and I found out what had happened. Until then he was described in the newspaper and hospital records as an "unidentified white male." I was angry and shocked. What kind of unfeeling monsters would do such a thing? Why would anyone target Rex, the gentlest soul in all of Cheyenne? It turned out the Cheyenne Police Department knew exactly what kind of creeps would do such a thing. They already had one attacker in custody for another offense. He was well known by the local police as a frequent flier in their jail. Based on the descriptions Rex was able to give from his hospital bed, the detectives recognized the suspect. When the police interviewed him, the thug confessed involvement and gave the name of his accomplice.

Gilbert DeMartine and Willard Newell assaulted Rex because they wanted money for drugs. Originally their plan was to rob a pizza delivery person but none was around so they picked up Rex instead. They knew he didn't have any money but decided to beat him up anyway. They had no remorse for their actions, only remorse at getting caught.

Rex looked so pale and frail in his hospital bed. His head was wrapped and his right eye and ear bandaged. I was nauseated, thinking of all the times he was pushed around at school by bullies. As I sat by his bedside, I flashed back to a day in high school when someone ran up to me in the hall at lunchtime and said, "Hey, you better go help your brother. He's in trouble," and pointed around the corner. I took off running and found him crouched down on the concrete floor in a ball, surrounded by a group of kids. A girl was yelling at him, telling him he was gross and should wash his hair. She had a cigarette lighter in her hand and was attempting to set his hair on fire to show what a 'grease ball' he was. When I rescued him his hair was singed on the edges, but thanks to a miracle, it hadn't completely caught on fire.

When DeMartine and Newell formally confessed to aggravated robbery (they took Rex's wallet) they bypassed a trial in the hopes of getting lighter sentences. I got a call from the Victim Witness Coordinator from the Laramie County District Attorneys' office telling me the date of sentencing if Rex planned to attend and make a victim impact statement. I wanted to go but Rex wasn't interested. Talking on the phone about the court date, I asked Rex, "But don't you want to tell the judge how you were hurt to make sure they stay in jail a long time?" He was quiet for moment and replied, "Well, it won't make my head feel better and the judge will do the right thing. My Best Friend told me to forgive them and I did. So I don't want to think about them anymore."

We were told one of the criminals would receive between five to twenty years in prison, the other would get a life sentence because he already had two other strikes against him and this was his third. Besides informing us of court appearances, the victim-witness assistance program also had a process to compensate crime victims for financial losses. Rex and his case manager filled out the application for compensation based on his permanent hearing and vision loss from the aggravated robbery. The Crime Victim Compensation Program is based on how much money you earn. A victim who worked and earned $10,000 a week could get that money back through the compensation program. Someone who earned minimum wage could only receive minimum wage back. And a non-employed, disabled person couldn't receive any money at all. Rex was denied assistance because he didn't have a job and they only compensated for lost wages not for pain and suffering. I understood the logic of the compensation, I just didn't like it. Knowing that money wasn't going to make his hearing or vision come back, I was hoping maybe he could at least get a new computer, like the kind with a big screen for the blind or good speakers to help compensate for his hearing loss. The whole thing was just so damn maddening. Rex had so very little in the world and it was unfair that the little he had was once again taken from him. And I was mad at myself. If I were a decent sister I wouldn't let him live alone so he wouldn't need to be out looking for someone to talk to at one in the morning. If I were a decent sister, I would be writing letters to the newspaper editors, letting all of Cheyenne know what those two criminals did to my brother. I would definitely be in court demanding the ultimate punishment.

When I told Rex how angry I was, he got a quizzical look on his face, like he was trying to understand. He quietly responded, "My Best Friend said not to worry about it. We don't have to be mad."

I didn't say anything, but after a moment my chest felt a surge of energy and I began to cry. Rex had a way of releasing me from my feelings of defeat and helplessness when I was unable to protect him. He didn't make me responsible for his suffering, even when it seemed obvious to me that I had failed him once again.

Rex wasn't interested in vengeance or retaliation. He just felt sad that he couldn't see from his right eye and he sometimes got dizzy or had headaches. Not hearing out of his right ear annoyed him. The most he would say was, "What? I didn't hear you out of that ear. It doesn't work good." Never mentioning the assault, or why his body didn't work right. No bitterness ever present in his voice.

Rex's capacity for forgiveness was truly limitless. In church, all my life I had been told we have to forgive. God judges, not us. Of course that wisdom was always prefaced with, "Christ is our example and he was able to forgive his trespassers perfectly. We, as mere mortals, struggle with forgiveness and it can often times take years to truly forgive. But keep trying. Someday you'll get there."

Rex was able to forgive as Christ forgave, without reservation and right away. He didn't forget the assault; he just accepted that he didn't need to think about it or feel bad. His Best Friend was taking care of it. He had the same perspective about his childhood sufferings and other wrongs he had been subjected to.

Shortly after we reunited in Cheyenne I tried to get him to talk about our early years. When I brought up the past with Rex, he studied my face seriously and said, "I don't want to talk about that."

"Why not?" I challenged, "The Spencer's did really crappy things to you."

"Yeah, but I don't think about that stuff" he replied. "My Best Friend says he took care of that."

I didn't understand who his Best Friend was at that time; Rex hadn't yet told us his story of walking from Utah and talking with Heavenly Father and Jesus Christ. I was irritated, thinking he just wasn't getting it. "I mean, bad stuff happened to both of us and it makes me really mad to even think about it. And I feel terrible when I think about what the Spencers did to you and how I couldn't stop it, you know?" I said, bracing myself for his angry reaction. I was prepared for whatever he had to throw at me.

I attempted formal therapy for myself several times, trying to rid myself of the demons from the past. Every day I burned with hate for all the evil things done to me, Rex and the other kids at the Spencers house. My rage about our years in foster care was nothing compared to the betrayal I felt from Harley and Virginia Spencer. They legally promised to love us. The foster home didn't. My therapy sessions never made it past the third or fourth visit. I kept running into the same brick wall I felt in group therapy in high school. Where do you even begin? I knew it would take years and years of talking before I would find peace, if I ever did. My insurance didn't cover therapy. Getting professional help for my pain was a luxury I couldn't afford.

I went to my bishop at church, asking for advice on how to forgive. He told me a story about how he was double-crossed in business and had to declare bankruptcy. It had been ten years since his financial reversal and his family was still struggling to replace what they had lost. He admitted he still had hard feelings towards the man who ruined him. He suggested I go talk to the people at a new therapy clinic housed in an evangelical church that advertised a Christian approach and they accepted love offerings in payment. It was odd a Mormon bishop would recommend another religion, but I figured it couldn't hurt. Therapy was therapy and as long as I wasn't asked to worship Satan, it would be fine. I called and made an evening appointment so Rob could watch our kids. Not having to pay for babysitting was a big deal because that doubled the cost of going to a counselor. When I arrived, I was greeted warmly by two women who were excited to see me. I was their first client. We sat on folding chairs and they listened as I gave them a short outline of my problem and asked my one question. How do I forgive?

They looked at each other for a moment and then one asked, "How did you find us?"

I explained my bishop at church gave me their flyer and said they might be able to help me. I needed a way to heal that wouldn't require me to dredge up my awful past, but how can you change the future if you don't acknowledge the past? I wanted a way to forgive my parents without spending decades of my life reliving it all again. Did they know how to do that? They flipped open the Bible and started giving me a lecture on Jesus's commands to forgive everyone and how I needed to turn my soul over to Him. I nodded in agreement, knowing they weren't real therapists. They were just church people trying to preach The Word. The same Word I heard my whole life in church. The Word even my bishop admitted he didn't know how to forgive the way Jesus said to do. If the bishop, a man of God, couldn't do it, what chance did I or these ladies have of doing it? After an hour of reading scriptures, they grasped my hands and in a prayer circle, they prayed the demons out of my heart and for Jesus to fill my heart with peace. I opened my eyes after they were done, recognizing their intents were pure, but they were in way over their heads. I thanked them for their time and gave them $10 for their efforts. The next time I saw the bishop he asked if I went to therapy and what I thought. He was considering sending others from the congregation. When I told him what had happened, his face went pale. He thanked me for going and said that he wouldn't be recommending that place after all. I told him I thought that was for the best.

I just couldn't see how anyone could offer me better advice than I was already getting. If talking alone could fix it, people like Mr. Gross would have healed me years ago. Of course, the fact Mr. Gross and other friends of mine had no idea of what happened to me and my brother probably explained why I always felt like I had a ton bricks on my shoulders.

Somewhere along my way of searching for relief, a friend pointed out that the only way to really heal a bad childhood was to give your children what you didn't get. That made sense to me. It was action. It was me actually doing something to change the direction of the river. More than anything I did not want to become like Virginia, whom I judged as a perpetual victim. I didn't want to tell terrible stories about my childhood to my children as an excuse for my poor parenting.

That brought me to my next problem. I didn't have a clue how to raise a child. I knew what I didn't want, but how do you know what to do instead? I fell back on what had always worked for me, books. I collected a shelf full of parenting books. I watched other families who I considered to be successful. I asked girlfriends how they handled things.

One of the best things I ever did was to enroll in an eight-week parenting class at the local community center. I was astonished the first day of class to find out I was the only non-court-ordered parent in attendance. It hadn't occurred to me that people who messed up in their parenting had to get training from somewhere. By accident I stumbled into an effective tool the local courts used. A tool that didn't require children to be put in foster care because of bad parenting. I humbled myself and admitted to the group that I hadn't done anything legally wrong as a mother, I just didn't know what to do. I decided I couldn't feel superior to the rest of the group because it was by the grace of God I hadn't repeated the same patterns of abuse and neglect I suffered as a child. I read the required parenting material and participated in the weekly group discussions. It really did help to see that I wasn't the only one struggling to know how to sanely raise children. It also gave me a shot of confidence to realize that compared to some of my classmates, I was doing pretty darn good in the parenting department. It's a shame that each child isn't born with its own personalized owner's manual. I knew more about how my dishwasher worked than I did about how to stop a kid from throwing a temper tantrum.

By practicing being the kind of mother I wished I had, the miracle slowly happened. I closed my eyes at stressful times and imagined myself from my children's point of view. How would I want my mother to understand me? It wasn't hard for me to remember what it felt like to be a powerless child. In many ways I still felt that way as an adult.

One of the most difficult things for me to overcome and yet the most necessary, came about as the result of a fad. During the early 1990's while my children were still very young, bumper stickers on cars were all the rage. Most cars had at least one sticker pronouncing an opinion on something. One day while driving I read my first "Have You Hugged Your Child Today?" bumper sticker. It hit me like a ton of bricks. I hadn't. Not only that day, but I couldn't remember the last time I touched any of my children beyond the necessary touching required in child rearing. I couldn't recall ever reaching out impulsively and hugging any of them. If they came to me for comfort I hugged and kissed them. I wasn't harsh in any way. I just wasn't naturally a touchy-feely kind of person. As I thought about it, I realized it was because I was never touched as a child beyond basic care or abuse. No one kissed me and tucked me into bed. No one said, "I love you, have a great day," as I went out the door to school. In the foster home and certainly not at the Spencers, was touching ever accompanied by anything remotely resembling honest affection. When I realized I wasn't hugging my kids the way a good mother would, I resolved to change that. It was difficult. I had to write notes to myself to remind me to do what didn't come naturally. I was sad that I didn't instinctively have the impulse to grab them up and squeeze the stuffing out of them. It was another reminder of how neglected my childhood really was. Luckily, Rob was an affectionate father and husband and by paying attention to how freely he cuddled and touched us, it was easier for me to remember to do the same.

It was hard and took years but I gained confidence in myself and was now able to reach out and help Rex with the major pain I knew he had to have. Rex didn't react to my offer of emotional support the way I thought he would. Not the way I would have. He paused, and said quietly, "Oh, I know. You feel bad about the things that happened to us. You want to fix it. You don't have to feel bad about it. I'm not mad, so you don't have to be either. They don't matter anymore and we don't have to fix anything," He patted my arm and that was that.

16. REX COMES HOME

For the record, cancer sucks. Brain tumors suck. And when someone you love gets a cancerous brain tumor, it really, really sucks. In 1998 Rex was diagnosed with this exact thing after having weird symptoms for a while. Earlier that year, he complained of a constant headache. Then he told me he felt dizzy and that food tasted fuzzy. He was tired a lot too. I dismissed his symptoms as being problems resulting from his assault. He went to Bishop Carmen and told him something wasn't right in his head. Dr. Carmen checked him and said he was fine. Rex could talk, didn't complain of pain that aspirin couldn't help and he passed a general physical.

Within a month of his check-up with Bishop Carmen, while riding on the city bus, Rex had a grand-mal seizure. He was taken to the emergency room at the hospital. They listened to his complaints and did an MRI to double-check his head. The tumor lit up like a Christmas tree. We got a call from Bishop Carmen, telling us the diagnosis. We were all shocked. Dr. Carmen apologized, saying he just didn't see the symptoms pointing to anything serious. I could tell he felt very badly about missing Rex's diagnosis. He had a stage three gemistocytic astrocytoma brain tumor. Surgery was scheduled to remove what they could, then radiation to shrink it. It was terminal. There was no way to cure it. The radiation treatment was to give him more time. The surgery happened within days. While Rex was recovering in the hospital, Rob, his caseworker and I recognized there was no way he could stay in his apartment and take care of himself. The regime of medications alone was daunting, not even counting dealing with feeling like crap, needing to eat decent food, not just ramen noodles and hot dogs and getting rides to doctors' appointments and radiation treatments. We decided the best thing to do was to move Rex to a nearby nursing home that had an excellent reputation and was willing to take him. His prognosis was six months, at most. His kind of tumor grew quickly and the timeline included the days added due to radiation shrinking the tumor temporarily. It was going to happen fast. Rex was 32 years-old. Rob and I drove up to Cheyenne the day before he was to be released from the hospital and told him our decision for him. He was not happy. He wanted to stay in his own place. He felt the people in his building needed him. He helped his elderly neighbors with carrying groceries, emptying the trash, moving furniture and whatever else they needed. After talking to him a while and telling him he had no choice, Rex lay back on the pillows and said, "Oh well. Maybe there is someone in the nursing home that needs my help."

I recalled his comment a short time later when Rob and I went to check out the nursing home. We were shown to the nursing director's office. Doctor Carmen had already talked to her and she was prepared with all the paperwork. She gave us the general information about the place and put the papers in front of us to sign. I asked, "Before we sign, would it be ok to look around?"

The director looked confused and said, "Sure, is there anything in particular you want to see?"

"Well, we just want to see his room and all," I shrugged. "It would make it easier for Rex if we all knew what to expect."

"Why, of course," she smiled. "Come this way," and she motioned us into the hall.

It was a clean, modern place with linoleum floors polished to a high shine, with floor-to-ceiling windows in the outer walls of the main corridor. We passed a room decorated like an ice cream shop, where she explained residents came every evening after supper to get a treat. "And we also have an old-fashioned popcorn cart on wheels for residents who love popcorn with our movies." She smiled brightly, showing us the large family room and big screen tv. "Movie nights are a big hit with our residents" she said.

"Rex loves ice cream and popcorn, so that's a real winner for him," I remarked.

We walked along the wide halls, moving amid the residents in wheelchairs, using walkers, and hanging tightly onto the handrail attached to the wall.

"My real concern is about Rex having a purpose. He will get bored very quickly if he doesn't have something to do and he will drive everyone crazy," I said.

"Well, we have chess games, card games, bingo every day, singing time three times a week…" she counted off on her fingers.

"No, I mean is there a job or chore for him to do? Playing games won't be enough for him. He will want to know he is helping," I explained.

"Hmm. I'll have to think about that. I'm sure we can find something, but my understanding is this won't be a ….long term placement," she said cautiously.

"Yeah, well, we really don't know how long it will be yet. But I know Rex, and having a purpose is critical," I said, taking a deep breath.

"I'm not worried about him, it's you and your staff and other residents who will be hounded to pieces if he doesn't have something to do. He needs to serve."

By then we arrived at Rex's room. The lights were down, there were two beds in the room. In the first bed near the door was the small form of a man's body under a thin blanket and sheet. He was sleeping, snoring softly. His face was relaxed and peaceful. He looked about a 100 years-old.

Next to the bed on the other side of the room was a window overlooking a fenced side yard. Each person had a tiny, two-foot wide wardrobe and two drawers for personal items. There was a bathroom in the room for them to share.

The room was the size, shape and color of a typical hospital room. As soon as I saw the room I realized Rex would be miserable here. There was no table for craft projects, no room for his filing cabinets, and no outlets for his computer and printer. What would he do all day? Where would he put his model car toys, favorite books, and Disney movies? There was no place for any of his things, especially since the nursing home rules wouldn't allow boxes stored under the bed. I felt terrible. As we walked out of his room and headed back to the director's office, her prattling on about resident-aide ratios, my mind was racing.

"What I am I going to do? Rex can't stay here. But he can't live alone. But he can't live with us. Rob would never go for it. We don't have room for him and he is a full-time guy even when he is healthy. I am trying to go to school, Rob is working crazy hours at his job and we can't afford to have him with us. What am I going to do?"

By then we were back at the door to the nursing director's office. I put my hand on Rob's arm and said, "Hey, before we sign the papers, would it be alright if we went and got something to eat? I'm starving and I'm afraid I'll get a headache if I wait any longer to eat."

Rob looked at me and said, "Sure, I guess we could go and eat."

We turned to the nursing director who was visibly annoyed.

"Well, I do have other things to attend to. I was planning on getting this done first, but it is your choice," she said very formally.

"Great!" I said. "We'll go grab a bite and we'll be right back."

Rob and I left and found a restaurant nearby. As we slid into our booth, Rob said, "So, what did you think of the place?"

I didn't answer, not knowing what to say. As the waitress handed us menus he pressed once again. "Well, what did you think?"

No way was I going to suggest what I was thinking. I

didn't have the energy to deal with Rob having a strong reaction to my thoughts, on top of everything else. So I said, "You tell me. What do you think?"

Rob sat quietly, studying the menu, and then he said, "Well, what do you think of Rex coming and living with us?"

I felt a rush of relief flow through my body. Rob had the same feeling of foreboding that I had in the nursing home. We talked and confirmed our decision, ate our meal hurriedly, and raced to go find Rex's doctor/bishop to tell him our thoughts. We found him working late at the church. We entered his office and explained our impressions. He was shocked. He expressed his concern that we were taking on way more than we could handle. He tried to reassure us the nursing home was very nice and they would take good care of him.

Rob said, "No, it's not about the nursing home. This is a strong feeling that we need to take care of him. That he needs us."

And so, against his doctor's advice, against the opinion of his case manager at the community mental health center, and anyone else who knew Rex, we made our decision. They all based their opinions solely on what they knew about Rex, but in the end they agreed. If they knew what Rob and I were dealing with at our home they might have been even more reluctant about letting him go.

Our three children, Jennifer, 9, Elise, 7, and Ty 4 were a handful. All three of them were born with moderate hearing losses. They wore hearing aids; the girls had special help at school and hours of extra speech and occupational therapy at the local hospital. All of them had extreme food allergies and I had to be careful of what they ate. Jennifer had a secondary learning disability; Elise had been diagnosed with epilepsy at two years-old and also had major problems with her bowels and bladder. The icing on my already stressed cake was Ty. He was severely allergic to foods, pollens and chemicals, making him excessively hyperactive and sickly. He never took naps, slept fitfully at night and it wasn't unusual for me to be up all night and all day with him.

Rob wasn't doing much better than me. He was over-worked, underpaid and just as stressed as I was about our family situation. Both of us had been under extreme pressure for many years; trying to figure out how to meet the needs of our children, our family and ourselves. It was not pretty and some days it was really ugly. We had high hopes that when Rob graduated and could just work one full-time job, our lives would be so blissfully easy, but it didn't seem to be working out that way.

In the months before Rex came to live with us, Rob told me to stop calling him at work because every time I did it was bad news about one of the kids and he couldn't get his work done. He was worried about his job and really needed to concentrate so he could be more than just the 'new hire.' I would have taken his attitude personally but I knew what he was saying. I just envied him that he could escape the chaos at home by going to work. I didn't have anywhere to hide. No wonder everyone who knew our situation thought we were crazy for taking in Rex, too.

When we went back to the hospital to share the good news that Rex wasn't moving to the nursing home, we found company in his room. It was a young couple both dressed in cowboy finery, ala Dale and Roy Rodgers. They were obviously good friends of Rex's and we didn't want to interrupt their visit. They were telling him about their plans to chuck it all and live out of their truck while following the pro-rodeo circuit. The husband had aspirations of being a professional bull rider and his young wife thought that was wonderful.

Within a short time it was apparent this couple had learning deficits and were being heavily guided by both sets of parents. I started to interject myself into the conversation, wanting to point out the foolishness of walking away from their trailer and jobs when they had no money and no other resources. Rob pulled on my arm to get me to shut up and I took his cue.

I watched in amazement as the agitation and frustration poured out of the couple. They began talking about how hard it was having their parents still telling them what to do. They were married and felt ready to take care of themselves. Rex didn't say anything, he just let them talk. He nodded occasionally and plucked at the bed sheet he lay under. After they had finished speaking, they both beamed and thanked him for his wonderful advice. They turned to us and she said, "I don't know what we are going to do without Rex to help us out. He is such a good friend and always gives us such good advice. We just love him to pieces."

Her western twangy accent drawled out on p-i-e-c-e-s. I wondered exactly what advice he had given. I hadn't heard any.

After they left in a flurry of swinging fringes and big cowboy hats, we told Rex we would be taking him home with us. I was expecting him to be really excited, like I was. Instead he argued to stay in his apartment, stating the people there needed him. We compromised, agreeing to keep his apartment until we were sure it was going to work out and he could come back at any time he wanted. The next day we packed his computer, toys and clothes, leaving everything else in his apartment and Rex moved into our home.

17. LET THE LEARNING BEGIN

The first morning at our house Rex came to me bright and early and told me he was fine being with us because he talked to his Best Friend. His Best Friend told him he was needed at our house and that in particular, he needed to help me with my family. It was about 6 a.m. when Rex reported this to me. I was dealing with crying kids who needed to get ready for school and the last thing I had time for was to humor his need to be important. I said something superficial and brushed past him to begin another day in the rat race I called my life.

Rex began a daily ritual right away. Every morning he waited outside our bedroom door until I came out. He learned to wait at our door after the morning I almost bit his head off for waking us up by knocking as soon as the sun was up. Every morning he told me that he talked to his Best Friend the night before. His Best Friend said he should play with the kids or help me with household chores or offer to help sort laundry. Every day it was a different assignment, but the source of the directive was always the same, his Best Friend. At first I played along, saying I would appreciate any help he could give, knowing that Rex was more like one of kids, rather than a help. He didn't know how cook or clean and often just followed me around the house, talking my ear off.

The kids adored him, especially Ty, who was four years-old. Rex and Ty had a lot in common. They both liked superheroes and watched cartoons together. They played with Rex's extensive Lego collection and Ty's Hot Wheel's cars. A favorite activity was watching a movie called, "Seven Brides for

Seven Brothers." In this classic musical, one scene portrays the socially backwards brothers kidnapping women to marry. One day as that scene was on the tv, Rex turned to Ty and said, "You know, we can't do that in real life. We would go to jail. No one is allowed to catch girls."

Ty nodded solemnly in agreement. Good thing the boys were grounded in reality.

Getting married was something Rex talked about. During one of his hospital stays, this one because I accidentally fed him a vegetable lasagna that had lima beans he was highly allergic to, he found one pretty blonde nurse irresistible. He proposed marriage if she would join the LDS faith. Apparently this proposal was much more intense than the typical male patient flirtation, and we had to explain Rex's condition before she was willing to work with him again.

I went into Rex's room, where he was cheerfully watching cartoons. "Hey, Rex, I understand you found yourself a wife. How did that happen?" I casually asked.

"What?"

Rex's eyes began blinking fast, a sure sign he was confused and nervous, thinking he might be in trouble.

"I heard that you asked one of the nurses to marry you. Did she accept?" I gently teased. "I don't know. All I did was tell her that if she was a Mormon we could get married. And if we were married it could be forever, even after we died we would still be together," he replied, sinking back into the pillows.

"So why do you want to get married?" I asked. "It's a lot of work to be married, you know. You have to be nice and always think of what the other person would like."

Rex rolled his eyes and sighed. "I know that. I am nice. And I always think of others. Aren't I good at your house? I help out. I clean my room and give you my dirty clothes. I try to help the kids not fight with each other. I am nice to everyone. I love everyone. You know that," he smiled, waiting for my agreement.

"Yes, you do love everyone. We should give you a new name, Dr. Love, because you are a love machine," I said, giving his arm a squeeze.

Rex laughed, his eyes brightening. "I am Dr. Love. I love everyone, just like my Best Friend said."

Thus was Dr. Love invented.

It tickled him so much to be thought of as a doctor of love, healing everyone with love, that from then on he introduced himself to everyone he met at as "Rex E. Spencer, Dr. Love." When he was home from the hospital he created business cards on his computer with his name Dr. Love, which he passed out happily to men and women equally. He wasn't talking about romantic love. He was talking about the love his Best Friend wanted him to share.

In the early days of Rex joining our family, I witnessed a temper tantrum like from our early childhood. Just like when he was four years-old, it was borne out of frustration with not being understood. Rex was doing something and Rob wanted him to stop. Rex ignored Rob's request, forcing Rob to speak louder and more directly. Rex still didn't respond. Rob went to him, touched his shoulder and said, "Hey, I said to stop that. You need to quit."

Rex looked at Rob, clenched his fists and stomped off to his bedroom, slamming the door. That escalated the situation. Rob wasn't about to ignore that behavior. "Rex, you better open this door right now. I'm not kidding. You don't just throw a fit when you don't get your way. And no one slams doors in my house," Rob was practically yelling through the closed door. "I'm counting to three and you better open this door."

Within two counts, Rex stood in the open doorway, his face red and eyes full of tears, with defiance on his face.

"Rex, I don't know what your problem is but don't you ever act like this again or I'll send you right back to Cheyenne and you can live in that nursing home," Rob said, his voice full of anger.

Rex responded by saying, "Fine. Do whatever you want. I don't care. I don't need you or this stuff," he motioned angrily to his computer and personal things. "I don't need any of it. Nothing means anything to me."

Tears of frustration streamed down his red, contorted face.

Rob stepped right up to him and jabbed his chest. "You will not be throwing tantrums in front of the kids and scaring them. You will find a better way to deal with your anger or you will be leaving. You decide." Rob turned to me and said, "I'm not kidding. We are not living with that behavior."

I was speechless. What the heck happened? I was in the kitchen making dinner and the next thing I know Rob is threatening to throw Rex out and Rex is daring him to do it. Didn't we talk about how we shouldn't yell at Rex and how we needed to be loving and patient and then Rob goes ballistic over some little thing? What was I supposed to do now?

Rex spent the rest of the evening in his room with the door shut. The kids and I were quiet, staying clear of both Rob and Rex. I didn't say anything to Rob until that night after we had gone to bed.

"I don't know what happened tonight, but you did not handle that well. You know that the absolute worst thing you could do is threaten to kick him out. Rex has lived a whole life of uncertainty. He's not even here a month and you are ready to quit." I was furious and the more I talked, the more my pain of Rex being repeatedly abandoned came to the surface. "That doesn't help him, or me, or our kids. What message are you sending the kids, anyway? If they do something you don't like, they are outta here, just like Rex? What happened to all the stuff you told the kids about how Rex was going to live with us forever, and he is part of the family now? You acted just like the Spencers did with him. You probably ruined our only chance with him. Thanks a lot for nothing."

I turned away from Rob in bed, too upset to talk anymore. After a few minutes of silence, Rob sighed. "You're right. I blew it. I completely overreacted. But it scared me when he acted that way, because I don't know what he will do the next time he gets mad. What if he hurts one of the kids? What then?"

I didn't have a response, all I knew is we couldn't act out of fear. I was glad Rob could see the situation from my point of view. It helped to not feel trapped in the middle between my brother and my husband, but I didn't know what to do. I didn't sleep at all that night. The next morning I had no energy to fight. What ever happened with my brother, I would have to accept it.

Rex was in his usual position, standing in the doorway, waiting for me to exit my room.

"Hey Rex, how are you?"

"I talked to my Best Friend, and I am sorry I got mad. I shouldn't have done that. I want to stay here. I don't want to go to the nursing home."

His face was anxious and worried.

"Don't worry, Rex. We're not mad and you aren't going anywhere. Rob just overreacted. But you have to promise not do that again. It was really scary for Rob and the kids. We didn't know why you were mad. Next time, you have to use your words when you are upset."

I was talking to him like I reasoned with Ty and Elise when I intervened in a squabble over a toy. 'Use your words' was short-hand for talking things out, instead of going straight to physical violence. Rex agreed he wouldn't lose his temper again which I didn't believe for a second, but at least no rash actions would be taken that day. But Rex did keep his word, and never displayed any anger or frustration beyond mild annoyance again.

When it was proposed that Rex receive fourteen weeks of radiation to shrink his tumor, I was doubtful. It wasn't going to cure him. I was concerned about side effects. The oncologist told Rex he was young and strong and he wouldn't have any trouble with the treatments. The doctor was a very pretty lady and he appreciated her kindness. He chose radiation. I told him I wouldn't choose if for myself, but it was his body.

Within two weeks of starting treatment Rex's stomach was constantly upset. His hair fell out in the area his head was being zapped. He had nonstop headaches and lost energy to play with the kids, something he really enjoyed. He quickly put on weight as a side effect of the steroids he was taking to reduce inflammation in his head. Hospice was involved because the prognosis was he had less than six months to live. Radiation was not going to change that. Traditionally, Hospice is only involved if life-saving treatments like radiation are finished, but Dr. Carmen thought I needed the help right away. Half-way through the radiation series, Rex was admitted to the hospital for extreme dehydration and nausea. He was throwing up blood and couldn't eat anything. He had sores in his mouth and throat. I had had enough and told the doctors Rex was done with radiation. Rex didn't argue with my decision. He was just very confused because the pretty oncologist had told him it wouldn't make him sick and it did. I told him that sometimes doctors say things that turn out to not be true.

The day I told the hospital staff Rex was stopping radiation treatment, the oncologist contacted the hospital lawyer. She wanted to take us to court to force continued treatment on the basis I wasn't emotionally mature enough to make the decision to stop treatment and Rex wasn't smart enough to disagree with me. The oncologist wanted Rex's medical decisions to be assigned to the hospital physicians. I was furious. She didn't talk to us at all. Who the hell did she think she was, trying to force such barbaric treatment on my brother? Radiation wasn't going to save his life but his suffering was acute enough to kill him. She didn't give a flying fig about Rex and definitely didn't know anything about my maturity. It was unbelievable that we were going to court to fight over a dying man's right to choose not to suffer needlessly. And how were we supposed to pay a lawyer for this? My mind was off to the races and I wanted to scream. She was just one more person in a seemingly endless stream who were trying to hurt my sweet, defenseless brother.

The hospital patient representatives came to Rex's room and explained he couldn't be discharged from the hospital until the legal issues were resolved. I had no idea that kind of strong-arm tactic was even possible. Rex was to be held captive until the hospital decided they were ready to let him go. I was scared Rex would be taken away from us and forced to take treatments against our wishes. I wanted to weep from the sheer injustice of it all.

Thankfully, I had the sense to call the Hospice nurse. I told her what was happening. She got the Hospice lawyer involved immediately and he reminded the hospital lawyer that because Rex was enrolled in the Hospice program, we had the right to refuse life-prolonging treatments. Thank God we had Hospice on our side.

I was appalled that a doctor had the degree of arrogance to think she knew what was best for my brother. She didn't even know him. It also made me think of the scary power doctors can wield over parents. What if Rex was one of my minor children? Would he be put into foster care and forced to take the useless radiation treatment because I disagreed with how to manage terminal cancer? Rob and I had several intense conversations exploring the situation of children with cancer and physicians abilities to take total control of medical care, regardless of parental wishes. Scary stuff to ponder. We never went back to that hospital with Rex out of fear of what they would try to do the next time.

A few weeks after Rex's release from the hospital, a piece of mail arrived at our house that answered a few of my questions about why the oncologist insisted Rex continue radiation treatment. It was a bill from her office. She charged $14,000 for the initial treatment Rex received. I called and talked to the billing clerk, who mumbled an apology and said to ignore the bill, I shouldn't have gotten it. It was supposed to go to the state for payment. I suddenly had perfect clarity for her motives.

I thanked Heavenly Father for Dr. Carmen's wisdom in

getting us enrolled in Hospice from the beginning. They were a blessing in every way possible. Hospice nurses became the only contact we had with medical treatment and all of their efforts revolved around making sure Rex was comfortable and had the highest quality of life possible. We were incredibly lucky to have them support us in our decision to focus on the quality of Rex's remaining life, not the quantity. Besides, I was secretly convinced Rex would die from the effects of the radiation treatment long before cancer took him.

Rex still continued to tell me of his nightly conversations with his Best Friend. One morning when I came out of my room, he sadly told me he talked to his Best Friend about me. I asked, "Oh yeah? About what?"

Rex said, "I told him you worry too much and I don't know how to help you. I wish you weren't so upset all the time." When Rex said that, I lost my temper.

"Look Rex, you keep telling me not to worry. It is easy for you to say that. You don't have to worry about paying bills or fighting with schools or dealing with deaf kids. All you have to do is play your computer games and have fun. I have to get the kids up for school and I have to figure out what to feed all of you, all day long. I have to do the laundry and make sure everyone gets whatever medicine they need. I do all the paperwork, all the phone calls, all the repairs and all the appointments for everyone in this house. You're so worried about me? Why don't you tell your Best Friend if He wants to help me, get someone here to help me deal with this stuff. That's the help I need."

I huffed off to wake up the kids.

The rest of the day Rex was quiet and kept to himself. That was fine with me, I was grateful for the break. That night before he went to bed, he made a point of telling me he would talk to Best Friend about what I had said. He would see about getting help for me. I smiled and said, "Sounds great, Rex," thinking, "here we go again."

The next morning, Rex stopped me in the hall. "I talked to my Best Friend about what you said. He said there is

188

nothing I can do or anyone else can do to help you. He said He wants to help you very much, but you haven't talked to Him in a very long time. He misses you and wants you to talk to Him."

I froze in my spot. For the first time I realized he was serious about Jesus being his Best Friend. There is no way Rex could have known I hadn't prayed sincerely in months. We went to church, we read scripture stories to the kids, and we had family prayer and blessed the food before we ate. I taught a Sunday school class, I spoke in church. By every outside measure, I was a religious person. But on the inside I was scared for my kids' futures, worried for Rob's career and everywhere I looked there was pain and trouble. I was questioning where Heavenly Father was in our lives and why He was making us suffer. I had lost hope in the idea of a loving, all-knowing God who blessed us for our efforts at goodness. Rob and I were working our hardest to take care of our children but every time I turned around there was more bad news. We never had enough money and I saw no miracles on the horizon. I was in a state of chronic anxiety, worrying, "What will become of us?" Having children with special needs made it impossible for me to get a job. My full-time job was figuring out how to help the kids. I studied nutrition, health care, hearing loss, learning disabilities, special education law and applied for every possible program to help pay for therapies our health insurance didn't cover. Just dealing with the mountain of medical and financial documentation needed to prove our miserable plight was a full-time job in and of itself. I had no faith that Heavenly Father or any Higher Power was going to save me. I was completely responsible for our family and I carried my burden heavily. I complained to Rob about how hard it was but he was helpless to fix it. None of our friends knew how beat down and discouraged I was. It was impossible for them to understand our circumstance; their kids were healthy and thriving. I listened with envy while they prattled on about gymnastics and sports schedules as I silently calculated therapies for my kids. I kept up the façade of religious stalwartness because I had it once and I hoped someday life would calm down enough I could find God again. He was only for people with perfect lives, who had the time and energy to ponder deep things. I was trying to douse a house on fire with a small cup of water and I didn't have the luxury of pondering anything deeper than trying not to be consumed in the blaze. Until something changed, Heavenly Father and Jesus were just going to have to wait their turn.

When Rex told me that Jesus was waiting for me to talk to him, I broke down crying and gave him a hug. I thanked him for talking to his Best Friend for me. Rex hugged me back and told me not to wait to talk to Jesus, that He would help me right away. I took his advice. That night before I went to bed I had a long overdue conversation with Rex's Best Friend. I never questioned Rex's inspiration again.

Since there were no medical options left for Rex I decided to take him to the founder of the homeopathic school I attended. Homeopathy had helped my kids and maybe it could help Rex. We had nothing to lose by trying.

I didn't bother trying to explain homeopathy to Rex. I just told him we were going to see my friend Spencer Woolley, who might be able to help him. I couldn't find a sitter for my kids so they came along to the appointment. Within minutes of arriving at the office and introducing my brother to Spencer, the kids decided to go nuts all at the same time. Ty began crying for no discernable reason, Elise hit Jennifer for looking at her and they rolled on the floor in a cat fight. I reluctantly had to leave Rex with Spencer while I stayed with the kids in the waiting room, threatening them within an inch of their lives if they didn't knock it off. So much for my good parenting techniques.

After an hour's appointment, Spencer and Rex came out. Spencer explained that the cancer was very far advanced, was probably caused by exposure to high levels of pesticides and only God could intervene at this point. I asked where Rex could have been exposed to pesticides and Spencer explained that the particular chemicals that showed up in the testing were commonly used in widespread insect sprays on municipal lands, like parks and golf courses. Rex piped up and said he liked to walk in the grasslands on the edge of Cheyenne and one time an airplane flew over him, spraying him with a liquid. He couldn't remember if he took a bath to get it off or not. Knowing Rex, I bet not. Spencer also told me Rex was highly intelligent and that he had no emotional stress issues to resolve. Rex was at peace within himself and with his future, whatever that might be. I found a measure of comfort from the appointment, knowing that there wasn't some obvious thing I was overlooking that might really help.

Rex didn't say much on the ride home and I was trying hard not to be annoyed at the kids for making me miss the appointment. Some days having children made it very hard for me to feel like a good Christian.

The next morning, Rex caught me in the hall, bright and early as usual and said he talked to his Best Friend about his appointment the day before. "What did He say about it?" I asked, curious as to what the answer would be.

"He said it was good, and I should take the stuff you give me because it will help me feel better." Rex reported. "So, if you have anything for me to take, I will."

I was surprised. It hadn't occurred to me to pray about homeopathy. I had prayed for help and homeopathy was recommended to try, but I never thought to ask if it was good or not. For all the questions and controversy about if homeopathy really works or not, Rex had taken it to his Source and received his own answer. That was comforting to me; not only for his care, but also for the fact that Rob and I were sacrificing our time and money so I could become a homeopathic practitioner. I was happy that I finally had something unique that I could offer my brother to help ease his suffering.

18. MOVING ON

Two months after Rex came to live with us the school district we were fighting with announced they had no intention of providing more services for Jennifer. We had a choice to make. We could take them to court or do as other families in our situation had done and move to a new school district. Our lawyer pointed out the expense and drawn-out process in fighting over special education rights. She questioned if we were in a position to proceed down this legal path. Stephanie's parents gave us the money for the lawyer's initial fees and we knew we couldn't afford any more legal challenges. We needed to stop fighting and move on. Court battles are reserved for the rich and that wasn't us. People like us count their pennies and see how far they can get to find another land of opportunity.

There was an excellent school for the hard-of-hearing in Denver, about 70 miles from where we lived. Rob worked in Denver and had been getting up at 4 a.m. every weekday to make his daily three-hour commute to work and then back home again. We hadn't moved earlier because we wanted to stay close to Rex in Cheyenne and we loved living in small town Windsor. Big city living and expenses never appealed to us. We decided since Rex being in Cheyenne wasn't a problem anymore, there was no reason to stay in a school system that didn't want us. The only problem was we had to live in Denver proper, inside the boundaries of that school district. Homes in that area were either outrageously expensive or located in scary, crime-ridden neighborhoods.

Rob and I spent weeks looking at houses in Denver while I was in hyper-drive, trying to keep our house ready for showings for prospective buyers. It is extremely difficult to sell a house when you have a person dying in it. The hospital bed, oxygen tank and table full of medicine tend to be a turn off to people looking for a new home. No one wants to think about funerals while inspecting your back deck.

After two months on the market, which at the time was a very long wait, our house went under contract. I was able to relax a little and concentrate on where we were going to live in Denver. Our efforts were fruitless. We couldn't even afford to rent in a decent neighborhood. Every Saturday for a month Rob and I arranged for people to stay with Rex and we farmed out our kids to friends so we could go look at houses. Finally it was the Saturday morning before we had to move out of our house. Discouraged and scared, Rob suggested we pray. We were sitting in the parking lot of a convenience store when we petitioned the Lord to send us help. We had only one remaining day to find a place to live. We were closing on the sale of our house and we would have nowhere to go with three kids, a dog and a brother who was dying from a brain tumor.

After our prayer Rob decided to call his parents in Phoenix, Arizona and ask their advice. They had extensive experience with moving. Rob's dad had retired from the Air Force and they had moved constantly while Rob and his sisters were growing up. He called his dad's cell phone. His dad answered on the first ring, telling Rob the day before he and mom had a very strong feeling we needed help and they decided to get in the car and come see us. At 9 a.m. on that Saturday, Rob's parents were less than an hour away from where we were in Denver. We were overjoyed. We met with them in a diner to discuss our housing problem. They listened and calmed us down. We decided to call the realtor and review a list of homes we had previously rejected. By lunchtime we signed a contract on a home we discarded because it seemed to need too much work. Rob's folks pointed out everything it needed was superficial updates that could be done over time. Without their clear-headed advice and comfort, I don't know what we would have done. Their visit was truly an answer to a desperate prayer before it was even uttered.

The next day we showed Rex and the kids our soon-to-be new home. While touring the house Rex became extremely agitated. He told both Rob and I he couldn't live there. He didn't feel good being there and wanted to get out of the house as soon as possible. Because Rex reacted so strongly, I turned to the realtor and asked, "Is there a problem with the house? My brother doesn't like it and says we shouldn't buy it."

The realtor turned pale and said, "Well, the house is fine, but…" she trailed off.

I pressed harder, "We have a contract to buy it and I want to do that, but I need to know what is going on. I have to know how to deal with Rex."

It turned out the previous owners were an elderly couple who lived in the house many years. Both of them died there, months apart from each other. Their surviving son was selling it.

Once we knew that people had died in the home, we prayed a special blessing on the house, asking for only good and loving feelings to exist and for all other spirits to leave. After that Rex was fine and he lived contentedly there. Later on our new neighbors told us the previous owners were not happy people and no one was sad to see them leave. I can only assume Rex was picking up on their negative feelings.

Our new home was not only the only affordable home that didn't need extensive work, it also turned out to be located within the boundaries of a local church congregation where Bishop Carmen's sister lived. She was married to the Bishop of our new ward. Both the new Bishop and his wife knew Rex from visiting her brother, Dr. Carmen. Several other couples in the ward knew Rex from having family members who attended the same congregation in Cheyenne. He already had built-in friends and was able to keep his connection with his friends in Wyoming, too. Once we realized how specific our new house and its location were to meeting Rex's needs, we felt compelled to say another prayer of thanks to Heavenly Father for guiding us to exactly where we needed to be.

Rex lived with us in Windsor for six months before we moved to Denver. By the time we moved, he was taking a lot of medications. The medication regime was changed often, trying to find a balance of keeping Rex comfortable without making him feel drugged. His spine was hurting all the time and the assumption was the cancer was spreading. There was no need to do testing; his condition was what it was.

The Hospice nurses and volunteers were a gift to me. Along with a weekly volunteer who came to play chess, Monopoly or computer games, he had a hospice massage therapist come to ease his discomfort. Rex liked the massages and often would insist on giving anyone who would let him, a shoulder, neck or hand massage. He wanted everyone to get a massage because they felt so good.

The pain of seeing someone you love suffering is the worst feeling. I hate feeling helpless. I dealt with my feelings of powerlessness to help Rex in my own unique way.

Our children had a trampoline to play on in the back yard. They loved to jump on it but my motherly instincts told me it was bad news. One fall from the tramp could really hurt or even kill them. I decided to dig a hole and drop the trampoline in it, making it level with the ground and lessening any chances of injury. The trampoline was a big, family-sized unit. It wouldn't be easy and I didn't ask Rob what he thought. I just went out back and started digging in the middle of the yard. I was well into destroying the turf by the time Rob noticed my project. He shook his head in disbelief but decided to ignore my craziness. Even though he didn't think it was necessary to dig a hole for the trampoline, he didn't try to stop me. He was too busy dealing with work problems to worry much about my little project in the backyard.

For three months whenever the weather was good and I had the time and energy, I dug. It felt really good to use my muscles and it helped loosen my chronically tight shoulders and neck. It also helped me to work peacefully with no tv, radio or computer noise, just the sound of birds chirping in the surrounding trees. It gave me time to not think about suffering, death, and dying.

The problem was I didn't know what to do with the dirt from the hole. First I added soil to all the flowerbeds, doubling their heights. Then I took to dumping it in a neglected corner of the yard where grass didn't grow well. I deemed it my future garden plot. After I filled a raised garden bed, I started hauling dirt around front to create a flowerbed in the middle of our completely flat, treeless front yard. I had no idea how much dirt could come out of a trampoline hole.

I thought it was a smashing idea and Rob didn't protest as I continued making my piles. After a certain point I thought I had more than enough dirt out front and decided to go ahead and plant flowers on my new mound. I spent all morning grooming the soil and organizing my new plants into color groupings. Rob happened to stop by at lunchtime from work and he saw my efforts first.

"You know, hon, your flower thingy there has a funny shape to it," as he pointed to the new mound.

"What?" I said, "It does not. It looks great."

He said, "Well, from my view coming up the street it looked like the shape of a coffin. Maybe you should make it a little rounder and less long and thin."

I was completely annoyed because he had no clue about creativity. He was just a man, and a dumb one at that! Thinking my flowerbed looked like a dead person's grave. The nerve of him. I proceeded to ignore Rob's observation and planted all the plants on the mound exactly as I planned. That afternoon as the kids jumped out of the school bus in front of our house, the driver casually commented, "So who died? It looks like you got a burial plot going right there."

I dug up all the flowers that afternoon and doubled the dirt on the mound, turning it into an unmistakable circle. Even my attempts at stress relief perfectly mirrored what my biggest problem was.

I wasn't the only one suffering from the unrelenting pressure of knowing a train crash was coming, not able to stop the high-speed locomotive as it careened down the tracks. While I was digging my grief hole in the backyard, our family Bassett Hound dog, Canelle, lazed nearby on the grass.

Once a week when a Hospice volunteer came to play board games with Rex, Canelle and I took an hour long walk around the neighborhood. Bassett Hounds look all relaxed and low maintenance but in actuality they are hunting dogs and need to be walked a lot. As Rex's needs demanded more of my time, I just didn't have the energy to take Canelle on her daily walks. That didn't work for Canelle. She started slipping out of the house whenever the opportunity presented itself. I got calls from neighbors a few blocks over who found Canelle, read her dog tag and contacted me to say they had my dog. I met quite a few nice people because of Canelle.

One particularly hectic day, I lost track of the dog and didn't realize she was gone until dinner time. The phone rang and it was a neighbor just around the block telling me that Canelle showed up at their house at 9 a.m. and had spent the day napping on their living room carpet. She was fine but they remarked how odd it was she just came into their house and made herself at home. That is when I knew the stress in our house was getting to more than just Rob and me. It wasn't just that the dog needed to walk, she needed to get away from the unspoken pressure cooker that was our life. It is pretty bad when even your loving dog, who has patiently accepted years of ear pulling, over-zealous petting, loud kid noise and all sorts of chaos, needs a break from the rivers of pain and anxiety that flow through the doors of your home.

19. FOR MEDICINAL PURPOSES ONLY

Even after we stopped radiation treatments, Rex's stomach continued to give him trouble. I gave him supplements and green drinks made with every healthy thing possible trying to help ease his discomfort. Sometimes the waves of nausea kept him up all night. I mentioned to a friend how bad the situation was and he casually asked, "Have you considered giving him marijuana?"

It never occurred to me. I was in homeopathic school and thought myself a very open-minded person, especially when it came to alternative treatments. But illegal drugs? That was a whole new ball game.

I researched marijuana on the internet and asked a few discreet questions of people who would know about such things, and then thought, "What the heck. Rex is dying. The whole issue of addiction is moot."

I called my friend who suggested it and asked if he knew where I could get some marijuana. Within a week I had a delivery of weed in an herbal tea box to try. I put it in the kitchen cupboard, not sure what to do next. Do I make some cookies or brownies? Do I make a cigarette, or do I put it into gel capsules? I knew Rex well enough to know the cigarette wouldn't work. His conscience would never allow him to smoke. Not only would the weed be a problem for him, smoking in and of itself broke the Mormon health code, the Word of Wisdom, which forbids smoking, drinking coffee, caffeinated tea and alcohol.

I told Rob what I had in the kitchen cupboard and asked his opinion of how to proceed in preparing it. He was floored. It was one thing to talk philosophically about drug use for terminally ill people; it was another thing to have in your kitchen. I think he was flabbergasted I actually knew someone who could get it. He pointed out the reality that if we got caught, and there was a good chance of that, what with the parade of Hospice workers coming almost daily to the house, we would be putting our children's welfare at risk. After our fiasco with the hospital oncologist wanting to take legal custody of Rex's health care, he didn't trust anyone in the health field, not even Hospice workers.

I reassured Rob that nothing bad would happen. I checked with a friend in law enforcement and he said in our situation it would be ignored. No policeman would pursue an obvious case of medical need. They were interested in bad guys, not people with cancer. After Rob and I talked, though, I decided it wasn't a good idea to try. I was more afraid of Rex blabbing than anything else. I could just see him saying to a visitor, "Here, my sister made these cookies to make my stomach feel better. I bet they would help you too. Have one." I sadly gave back the "love offering" and ended my brief career in illegal drugs.

Our experiences with legal drugs however, were expanding daily. The Hospice nurse told me Rex's medication costs were putting a strain on their budget because he was taking expensive oral drugs and using pain patches. People are put in Hospice when the expectation is they will live less than six months. Rex had been with us for eight months, with no end in sight. His medical care was paid for through a combination of Medicare and Medicaid government funding but he was using far more resources than expected. I didn't know what to do with what the nurse told me. We weren't trying to keep him alive, we were just trying to make his life as comfortable as possible. I didn't know if she was signaling that Rex would be taken off Hospice because he wasn't dying fast enough, or if she was just making a general statement that my brother was unusual. I was too afraid to ask her for clarification, so instead I didn't sleep for a couple of nights, worrying how I could possibly take care of Rex by myself.

He got himself up every morning, took his own shower, worked on his computer and played with the kids. He wasn't bedridden. His pain was worsening, but he still insisted on going to church every Sunday, even if just for sacrament meeting. At church, he continued his pattern of shaking hands with everyone and asking if there was anything he could do to help them. It was almost like the formal church meetings were there just to give Rex the platform he needed for his work. Before and after meetings Rex would catch people in the foyer, give them a Dr. Love card, then point to me and say, "If you need anything, just call me at the number and my sister will take your message and she will give it to me. I will help you."

Most people smiled and took the card. One elderly lady, not knowing Rex at all, took him at his word and gave him a call. She asked for assistance with yard work. Rob fielded the call and arranged a work group from church to help her out. I had to laugh. Even when Rex was in too much pain to sleep at night, he managed to make sure everyone was taken care of.

Rex began complaining of not being able to breathe but the oxygen levels in his blood were good. He kept saying he was suffocating. Hospice provided him with oxygen for several months, which he used whenever he needed it. Then the pain meds were changed from pills and patches to an I.V. pump. That caused problems because Rex wasn't able to report when pain was better or worse, all he could say was that he was hurting. He couldn't distinguish between yesterday's pain and today's pain and couldn't rate his pain. No one knew how much medicine to give him. I learned to pay attention to his actions. When he was in high pain he couldn't relax or rest. He needed new crafts, new puzzles, a new movie, anything to distract himself from the pain.

One of the lessons Rex taught me was that there aren't any bad experiences in life, just experiences. When he was first diagnosed with a brain tumor, he told everyone who talked to him, "Well, now I know how it feels to have cancer."

It was a really weird thing to say when someone was trying to be nice and compassionate, like, "I'm really sorry you have a brain tumor. This is terrible. Is there anything I can do?"

People would be speechless and fumble and exit pronto when Rex would reply, "Well, now I know how it feels to have cancer."

I was freaked out by his response and tried to talk to him about it. "Ya know Rex, when people say they are sorry about the brain tumor it is probably the best thing to say something like, "Yes, this is quite hard. Thank you for caring."

He looked at me like I had twelve heads (who knows, with the residual problems from his assault and then the tumor, maybe I did have twelve heads to him.)

He asked, "Why would I say that?"

"Because people feel bad for you and want to help, but they can't fix this. So instead, they are just letting you know they care about you."

"But I am telling them the truth. I do know how it feels to have cancer," he argued. I gave up.

At a fast and testimony Sunday meeting, Rex made a beeline for the pulpit and grabbed the microphone. "I want to bear my testimony, I know the church is true and I know my Best Friend loves everyone one of you. And I love you, too. I have cancer in my head. And now I know what it feels like to have cancer. If you have cancer or know someone that does, could you please tell me, so I can help them? Since I know what it feels like, I can help them now."

Tears sprung up in my eyes and I took a deep breath. I was worried he wasn't showing any emotions about his diagnosis. Here I was thinking he was once again making inappropriate comments that made people uncomfortable. I was wrong. He viewed his situation as a learning opportunity and an opening to connect with others. He didn't have pity parties about anything. Maybe it wasn't physically possible. He didn't get stuck in the past, thinking of all the horrible stuff he endured. In fact, he referred only to the present and future.

On the rare occasion I felt emotionally strong enough to probe an old wound scabbed over, he refused to join me in a game of "Remember when that crappy thing happened to you and how did you feel about it?" He would just look me in the eyes, squint, cock his head to the side, as if he was trying to recall the past and say, "I don't really remember all that. And it doesn't matter anyway. Hey, did I tell you about my new business?"

20. NOT WHAT I EXPECTED

In December 1998, with Christmas coming, Rex once again focused on being Santa Claus; wanting to make sure every child got toys. I was anguished. That was the only part of his old pain that never went away. He got on the computer and found a new website that offered to help him file the legal documents for his latest non-profit corporation for worldwide toy distribution to children. It would make it easier for big companies to donate money. He asked me if I would pay the fee to have his paper work processed. I told him I didn't have money for that and besides that was the job of parents. He looked at me with sad eyes and sighed, "All right. I'll just have to do it another way."

I was heartsick that he fixated on Santa Claus, Inc. so much, but I was grateful he let it drop.

In mid-December, Rex's pain and exhaustion prevented him from attending church at all. I felt we didn't have much time left. I called Bishop Carmen in Cheyenne. He said he would be down in Denver to visit his sister's family in our neighborhood so he made plans to stop by. Rex and his old bishop visited for an entire afternoon, which picked up Rex's spirits immensely. Bishop Carmen told him everyone missed him and was praying for him. Rex talked about going back and visiting but he was just too tired now. They had a wonderful time and Rex was very happy to see his old friend.

Later that month, out of the blue, he told me he wanted to talk to the Spencers. He wanted to see how they were doing.

I hesitated, putting him off a few days hoping he would forget. But he didn't. After his fourth request I dialed the phone number in my address book. I didn't even know if the number was still good as I hadn't talked to them since we lived in Utah several years before. Other than sending yearly Christmas letters with pictures of my family, I had no contact with them. I hadn't told them of Rex's cancer or his living with me. I didn't see the point. They didn't care about him.

When I called, Virginia answered the phone. "Hello?" she asked.

I said, "Hi, this is Heather."

"Well, long time no hear. How are you?" She sounded surprised and yelled, "Dad, it's Heather on the phone," to Harley, who was somewhere in the background. Just hearing her voice made my whole body shake uncontrollably from anxiety. I just wanted this over with.

"I have some bad news. Rex has cancer in his brain and is living with us now. I thought you should know."

That was a lie; I didn't think they should know anything but it softened the whole topic as an introduction for Rex.

"He wants to talk to you and Dad." I said, and handed the phone to Rex. Rex put the phone to his ear and answered softly, "Yes, it is me. I am here. Yes, I am fine. The doctors say I will die, but I don't know." He listened for a long time. He finally said, "Yes, I have. I am ok," he said. "Well, it was nice talking to you. I love you too. Bye."

He hung up the phone and grimaced.

"What happened?" I asked.

"They asked if I had repented of my sins and if I had a relationship with Heavenly Father." He blew out a big breath.

"Oh," I replied. I didn't know what to say.

Who would respond like that when told their child had cancer and was dying? To even ask such a question confirmed they didn't know Rex at all. It was interesting their only concern about Rex had to do with his being right with God. After I thought about it, I realized I should have expected that kind of response. Reflecting back over our lives, I remembered the way Harley and Virginia locked Emelia in her room for months with only the scriptures to read. And how they did the same thing to Madeline and McKenzie, telling them to read scriptures until they could forgive their dad for sexually and physically abusing them. They never dealt with anything with love or compassion. It was always an abstract, twisted religiosity that made no sense and turned God into a monster. That was the last time Rex mentioned the Spencers. They never called or made contact either.

During the month of January it was becoming much harder to keep Rex comfortable. He was frantic, constantly needing to be doing something to keep his mind off the pain. The previous month he stopped going to church and now just stayed home. But he wasn't sick in bed, too weak to move. Rather, in too much pain to lie around, his only comfort was his computer and numerous craft and toy projects.

Near the end of January when he had to go back to the hospital for pain control, Rex became angry. "I don't feel good and no one is making me feel better," he complained.

"I know Rex. The doctors are doing everything they can," I said.

The Bishop and Rob gave Rex a blessing of comfort while he sat propped up in the hospital bed. They laid their hands on his head and said a prayer blessing him with peace. Rex cheered up after they finished the blessing.

The next day I brought to the hospital the homeopathic remedies he was taking to help with his constant digestion problems and restlessness. One of the doctors saw the remedies and was annoyed. He told me the homeopathics were the reason Rex was miserable. Of course! They were obviously the reason the prescription medicine wasn't working. The doctor said they couldn't do anything more. With the homeopathic remedies being used, Rex just needed to be discharged. Despite the fact he was on a 24-hour I.V. drip for pain and 12 other pills I couldn't even keep track of, the whole problem was obviously a simple, over the counter homeopathic remedy to help Rex relax. What an asshole. I was at the end my patience with stupid, arrogant doctors.

Rex was upset he was being sent home when he still didn't feel right, and I had to say, "Rex, the doctors can't fix this. They don't know what to do. You are taking all the medicine they have." He grumbled about how that wasn't right at all. I had to agree. We went home.

That evening, Rex seemed to rally. He had enough energy to work on his computer and asked for help with a new business idea raising money for his Santa Project. I thought, "Here we go again. Christmas just ended and he's already thinking about next year."

I agreed to look at his idea in the morning because it was getting late. That night I could hear Rex moving around in his room, going from his computer to tv and back. His vision was bad enough he had to be right in front of the screen to see anything. Before 6 a.m. the next morning, I heard loud banging coming from Rex's room. As I shook off the fog of sleep I thought, "What is he doing in there?"

I heard a strangled sort of yelp. I immediately reached for Rob and we rushed into his room. Rex was in his bed, having a grand mal seizure. He was crying out in fear. His whole body was violently shaking. His body was flailing so furiously he was going to fall off the bed and hurt himself. We grabbed him and slid him off the bed and onto the floor. Rob and I tried to hold him and comfort him, but the seizure wouldn't stop. I left Rob with Rex and ran to the kitchen phone to call the Hospice nurse. I told her what was happening and asked her to come right away. She said she would, but it would be at least 40 minutes because she lived across town. She asked me what I wanted to do. I told her I wanted to call the ambulance. She pointed out Rex had just been discharged from the hospital the day before and there wasn't anything new they could do. I said, "Yes, but at least they could give him something to stop this terrible seizure."

She agreed with that and I hung up to call 911.

After I called the ambulance I went back to Rex's room.

Rob was sitting on the floor, holding Rex's upper body in his arms as his body was shaking in waves of convulsions. In the short time between the seizures Rex was praying, not a rote prayer, but more having a conversation, saying, "Make this stop. It hurts so much. I just want it to end. Please help me, Father."

Time slowed down and everything seemed to take hours. Rex's seizure didn't stop, the ambulance didn't come, I waited in a vortex, things swirling all around me, yet I was standing frozen in the middle. I willed myself to move, not allowing my mind to shut down. I went back to Rex's bedroom. I kneeled down next to Rex and Rob. I stroked Rex's arms and torso. I said, "The ambulance is coming. They will take you to the hospital and make this seizure stop. I love you. You are the best brother in the whole world and I am very proud of you. I am glad I am your sister. You are a great man, Rex and I will love you forever."

Tears streamed from my eyes and dripped freely on my face. I couldn't remember the last time I told my brother I loved him or if I had ever cried for him. I just wanted him to know that I did care about him, even if I couldn't stop his suffering. I heard the sirens in the distance and ran to the front door to let the emergency team in. The first to arrive were firemen. I pointed down the hall to Rex's room and continued to wait for the ambulance at the front door. There was a lot of banging and moving furniture around in Rex's room. Four of the firemen quickly pulled Rex down the hall, into the living room where I was standing. They spread out and started barking orders to each other, opening cases of equipment. Rob came to me and hugged me, shielding my face from Rex.

"He's gone. He's gone," he whispered in my ear.

I didn't understand. I pulled back and realized what Rob was saying when I saw the firemen preparing to use electric paddles to shock Rex's heart. I broke away from Rob, ran to the kitchen, where a 'Do Not Resuscitate' order from the hospice program had being hanging on the refrigerator door for months. I never expected to need it.

It wasn't supposed to be like this. We were supposed to know the end was coming. The Hospice team would tell us time was short and I would call Cheyenne so Bishop Carmen and President Skipper could drive down. I would greet them at the door with fresh homemade cookies and milk. I would be grateful for their company and support. We would all gather around Rex's bed and be able to tell him one by one how much he meant to us. My kids would get to see him and he would squeeze their hands. It would be late in the afternoon when we would tell Rex it was time for him to leave us and go to his Best Friend. The sun would be filtering through his window blinds, spilling across his white sheet and blanket. Rex would smile and tell us he loved us, too. He would close his eyes and fall asleep. After a few breaths he would be gone. We would all hug and cry and the Hospice people would make hushed phone calls. I would be sad but accepting that it was Rex's time to go. That is what was supposed to happen.

The monstrosity playing out on my living room floor wasn't real. It was in slow motion and right out of some terrible, second- rate movie. The grotesque hulking bodies of men hunched over Rex, pounding on his chest, the ambulance team standing at the door with a gurney in their hands (Where the hell were they 10 minutes ago?) Rob and I huddled together off to the side as witnesses to this crime. This Was Not Real. I shook off my haze and thrust the DNR paper at one of the firemen who were working feverishly on Rex. He glanced at it while preparing to do another round of chest compressions. "Whoa, what's this?" he asked.

I said, "It's from Hospice, Rex has cancer."

They stopped working on him. One of them muttered to the others, "Hospice? What the hell are we doing here?"

I didn't say anything, but what I wanted to say was, "Sorry for the inconvenience. I thought he was just having a seizure. I wasn't expecting him to die."

Instead, I cried.

It was over. My whole life of anxiety and fear for him. From my earliest days of feeling helpless to protect him and at the same time feeling frustrated because he just kept asking for trouble. Knowing I was a rotten sister for not being bold and telling every kid at school who picked on him to go to hell. For not boycotting Christmas presents as a sign of solidarity. For not sneaking food to him every day. For not packing my stuff and going back to Oregon with him. For not volunteering to have him live with my family and me years ago. For only being willing to take him in when God made my whole body sick at the thought of leaving him at the nursing home. For not giving up on trying to make him fit in and be normal. For being annoyed at the extra work he created for me. For losing sleep wondering who would take care of him as an old man if I died first. For worrying how much his funeral was going to cost and how I would pay for it. For wishing I could heal him and give him the life every person deserves.

On the day Rex died, the mail came early. I wouldn't have paid any attention to the reminder that life continued on as normal even when it obviously wasn't, but a special letter came that day. For a month previous to his death, Rex had been pestering me to order a copy of his patriarchal blessing from church headquarters in Salt Lake City, Utah.

A patriarchal blessing is given to members of the Mormon church by a man designated as an ordained patriarch. The blessing is personal revelation from Heavenly Father, given as a guide in this life to help identify strengths, weaknesses and eternal potential. The blessing can acknowledge the past, and tell of things to happen in the future, along with warnings and admonitions that will help that person. Each blessing is sacred and personal and is not to be shared with anyone outside the immediate family. A patriarchal blessing is eternal and its promises may extend into the next life.

Traditionally, one patriarch serves many congregations in an area, and may give blessings to a thousand people in his lifetime. He does not necessarily know the people beyond their name when they come for a blessing. Think of it like in the

Old Testament of the Bible, when a father would bless his son with a rich and happy future if he were obedient to God's will.

Rex was 14 when he received his patriarchal blessing. A typed copy of the blessing was sent to Rex and another copy was sent to church headquarters in Utah to be kept in the official church records. When Rex was sent away at 16 years-old, his copy of his blessing stayed in Arizona with Virginia and Harley. Rex had forgotten what his blessing said and he wanted to know what Heavenly Father had told him as a young man. After a week of Rex's constant reminders, I called church headquarters to request a copy of his blessing. They politely explained I couldn't request his blessing, only Rex. It had to be in writing with his signature. It could take up to 8 weeks to receive the document in the mail. I understood the whole guarding privacy thing but it was just one more hassle to deal with. After another week of Rex's badgering I finally typed a letter requesting a copy of his blessing and had Rex sign it. I told him it was in the mail and to not bug me about it because it would take a long time to get a response back. Only it didn't take long. It arrived on the day he died.

One paragraph leapt out at me, as if it were in bold print:

" I bless you, Rex, that you may have the inner peace and satisfaction which comes from knowing that as a child of God that He loves you and is mindful of your needs, and if you will pray to Him and seek His help, it will be given you to have the spirit of the Holy Ghost to be and abide with you and you will have a firm assurance of the love that our Father in Heaven bears for you...I bless you, Rex, that if you will be prayerful, our Father in Heaven will bestow upon you the gift of the Holy Ghost in rich abundance, that you will have the assurance that in making decisions that are difficult that the spirit of our Father in Heaven is with you to guide and direct you in the way that you should go, and the gospel will become a

lamp unto your feet and a light unto your path, that as you walk through life you may sense that you have the companionship of the gift of the Holy Ghost to be and abide with you, to lead you through life so that when you have completed your sojourn upon the earth you may depart without fear or trepidation, assured in the knowledge that you have fought the good fight, that you have earned the blessings that are in store for the faithful."

Receiving my brother's patriarchal blessing on that day confirmed to me that the message of the blessing was meant to comfort me, not him. Rex knew that he was loved by God. I was the doubting one, the one who struggled to let go of the pain of the past and to forgive myself for my failures as his sister. The realization that this blessing was given to Rex when he was 14 years-old, long before he would have the spiritual experiences that would make the blessing literally true for him, made me want to weep with relief. There was an Eternal Plan after all. God knew Rex and had prepared for his life, terrible as it was, from the beginning. Rex was loved, even when it wasn't by me.

21. HOW SWEET IT IS

Rex had every right to be a serial killer. The world would have understood given his early years that it was inevitable that he would become a cold-blooded criminal. But he didn't. He chose to go the opposite way. Not because he received world-class therapy and intensive professional help. He didn't. His life was lived on the streets of America and his heart healed its pain one person and one prayer at a time.

His funeral was held the following week in Cheyenne. I didn't call the Spencers to tell them Rex had died. I was fearful they would show up and do the whole grieving parents act and I just couldn't let that happen. I didn't have the stomach or the strength to defend Rex from them even in his death. I did get a few surprised comments from people who thought I should have invited our adoptive parents. It hurt to realize I was being misjudged as cold-hearted and unfeeling at the very moment I needed the most support. I could only comfort myself with Rob's reassurances I was doing the right thing and that those who questioned my decision had no knowledge of the pain and destruction the Spencers had heaped upon Rex.

As I walked into the chapel in Cheyenne, I was surprised to see the whole room full. People came from our town in Windsor, Colorado, from all over Cheyenne and one couple drove from Idaho to attend his services. I didn't recognize most of the people and wondered how they each knew Rex. There were at least 200 people there. It was truly amazing. Rex had lived a life of suffering, poverty, despair and homelessness.

He had been marginalized in society and had fallen through every crack possible in every system. Who were these people who came to pay their respects to him? They took time out of their lives to come together and show support for a man who had only known love for the last five years of his hard life.

When the obituary notice was read aloud at the beginning of the service, I had to smile. When I called in the obituary information to the newspaper a few days after his passing, they asked me his name, birth date, and death date. Then I was asked what his occupation was. I was stumped. Rex didn't have a career. He didn't even drive a car. I told the person Rex was unemployed. She insisted that would not work for the obituary. An occupation had to be stated. I remembered one of the last official jobs Bishop Carmen helped Rex get before he got sick was selling a roof sealant commonly used on mobile homes. It was a multi-level marketing home-based business. He never sold more than two gallons of the stuff. In his official death notice it read Rex worked as a salesman for an oil refinery. I guess death notices are one of the few times a mediocre job can be made to sound great. I only wished I was thinking straight enough at the time to say his true occupation: Rex Ezra Spencer, a lifetime of world service as Dr. Love.

Rex was buried in Cheyenne. At the time he began Hospice care, the counselor asked Rex what his wishes were for his body. He didn't understand the question. She delicately rephrased her request and Rex said, "Oh, I don't care. It doesn't matter what you do with my body after I die. I won't need it again."

The Hospice counselor asked, "Would you like to be cremated?"

Rex didn't understand that question either and replied again, "You can do whatever you want. I don't care what happens to my body."

I interrupted and said, "Rex, cremation is where they burn your body and then the ashes are buried. Is that what you want?"

Rex looked at me and at then the Hospice counselor in

horror and said, "I don't want to be burned up. That would hurt. I would be afraid." Rather than try to explain the realities of cremation, I told the counselor we would prefer a traditional burial.

A few days after the funeral, we held another memorial service in Denver for people who couldn't attend the services in Cheyenne. Once again, I was surprised at how many people came. Rex only lived in Denver nine months, but he managed to touch enough people to fill another chapel.

At that service, Rob spoke of his relationship with Rex.

"Rex came into my life as a stranger. Then he became my brother-in-law. Then he became my friend. Then he was my brother. Before he died, as I held him in my arms, he was my child."

I sat in silence for a moment after Rob said that. I didn't expect it and had no idea that was how Rob felt. He never told me that. Then I burst into tears. My husband loved my brother as his own child. I couldn't imagine Rob saying a more beautiful thing.

I Rex Ezra Spencer to state that if I die all that I have belonges to Heather Spencer Young and it's not my wish for Heather Spener Young to need to pay for any thing from me.

I am beging to set up funds to pay my death. If I die before that is done then drop me in an box and put my body any location you wish. Because I at death I have need only to know the location body was left.

After I dies you do not need to wory about me. Just remember I love you and everone forever. Spend your time and teach everyone what is real love so you can help me do my job from GOD.

The will of Rex Ezra Spencer

Sign of Rex Ezra Spencer

Rex E. Spencer

April 5, 1998

22. LIFE ALWAYS GOES ON

A few months after Rex passed away, Rob and I moved to central Illinois so our children could attend a special school for the hearing-impaired. It was a hard move so soon after Rex's passing and I was emotionally spent.

We loved Colorado but the needs of our children exceeded what we could access in the west. The special Deaf and Hard of Hearing program in Denver only went up to 6th grade and then the children were dumped into the middle of a large urban school. I remembered how scared I felt in the massive schools in Phoenix and thought my kids would be eaten alive in Denver.

It was hard to leave the people who knew Rex and appreciated him, but we had to do something different for our children. In our new home in Illinois no one knew my brother and the few times I tried to talk about him, the response I got was a blank stare. Everyone has loved ones who have passed away. My brother was no different than anyone else. It was as if I finished reading a book and closed the cover. That chapter of my life was over.

A year after Rex died the phone rang. I picked up the receiver and was surprised to hear a voice saying, "Hello Haddie. This is your mother, Claudia. How are you?"

I listened, my mind swirling like a lazy tornado as she told me she and Ralph lived in Temple, Texas and she been told that Rex had died. Was that true?

I told her yes and that he died from a brain tumor. There

was a pause on her end and then she said, "Well, we'll all be together in the Second Coming, so he will be fine."

I hadn't seen her and Ralph for over 10 years, not since we met in the parking lot at NAU and then they went on to Phoenix to give the Spencers lice. As I remembered Virginia calling me to complain about the lice, I smiled.

Claudia interrupted my inner laughter, saying excitedly "We've decided to move to be near our granddaughter. We are moving to Illinois next month."

I thought, "What?! I don't even know you people. Why would you come here?"

But I didn't say that. In fact, I didn't say much of anything. I was in shock. I did tell her I had two more children besides Jennifer and she asked me to send pictures.

I asked how they would pay for the move and Claudia explained they took out life insurance policies for Rex and me when we were born. When I got married they dropped me but kept paying a small annual premium on Rex's policy. They had received notice from the company of Rex's passing, and the insurance company tracked me down for them. I was surprised by Claudia's call and doubly surprised they had kept life insurance on us kids. They received money from Rex's policy and had a plan to get back into my life whether I liked it or not.

Within a week Ralph and Claudia were on our front porch. They looked older and Claudia had put on quite a bit of weight, but other than that they were the same people I remembered, including the poor personal hygiene. But what they lacked in clean clothes and fresh breath they made up with happy go-lucky attitudes. I didn't want them to stay at our house, so I paid for a motel room. I could tell they were disappointed, but no way was I going to jump into Crazy Land with both feet. I was going to go as slow as I possibly could.

After driving around our small town, their minds were made up. They were moving. Ralph and Claudia drove back to Texas to pack their things and I went into full panic mode. As

I told my friends the situation, several of them asked, "Why are you allowing them to come? Just tell them no. Tell them you don't want them around."

It hadn't occurred to me I had the power to do that. What was I going to do, bar them at the state line? They had money from Rex's life insurance policy to afford the move. They didn't ask me if I wanted them to come. They told me they were coming, they didn't ask my permission. And a part of me wanted them to come. I wanted to know about me and my brother, how we ended up in foster care and then were adopted. I wanted them to fill in the blank spaces in my imaginary baby book. I wanted the answers I had waited my whole life to get. I just wasn't sure what else I was getting in the bargain.

At first I was overwhelmed by the possibility of having to take care of them like I did my brother, but a dear friend gave me good advice that calmed my fears. She reminded me, "Your parents have lived for many years on their own and they managed very well. Don't take away their right to live as they wish."

So I didn't.

Even when I realized both my parents were full-blown hoarders, I kept my mouth shut and repeated the mantra, "It is their life. It is not mine. They have lived this way for longer than I have been alive. It is not mine to change."

As we slowly got reacquainted, Claudia told me the story of how she and Ralph met while working together at the Goodwill Thrift Store and were married at the courthouse in 1964. An uncle gave them the money for their marriage license and they bought wedding rings from a pawn shop.

After they married, Claudia petitioned the court to have her name legally changed from Janet Pogue, her birth name, to Claudia Wade, the name she gave herself after mental illness took hold of her psyche. Claudia's mother, Lennis, also went to court, arguing the judge shouldn't allow her daughter to change her name. Lennis contested that her daughter's name was

Janet. It was the schizophrenic illness that was requesting this change, not Janet. Her daughter wasn't an alien from another planet who called herself Claudia. Janet loved her mother and wanted to stay herself. To Claudia's satisfaction, the judge sided with her and told Lennis that Claudia was 21 years-old and if she wanted to change her name she could. Lennis lost whatever control she had over her daughter that day.

My brother was born a year after their wedding and Claudia named him Ezra after a great Jewish leader in the Bible. She knew from our conceptions that Ezra and I were destined for greatness. When I was born two years later, she named me Hadassah after the birth name of Queen Ester in the Old Testament. Claudia wanted us to have names befitting our importance as part Earthlings and part citizens of her home planet, La Mordia. We were unique in the whole world and she wanted us to remember that.

Claudia's obsessive need to keep every piece of paper came in handy a few months into our reunion. I was rearranging boxes in their crowded living room and Claudia asked, "Do you remember what your favorite fruit was as a child?"

I said, "No, I don't remember," and as I felt an inner welling of frustration, I sarcastically added, "I don't remember much about my childhood. But I expect you can tell me all about it," knowing full well I was only a weekend visitor in their lives.

Claudia didn't react to my sarcastic comment. Instead she rooted around in her metal filling cabinet and pulled out a large legal-sized manila envelope full of papers. As she handed the envelope to me she said, "Here, you can have this. I kept it so you could read it yourself."

I thanked her and slid the papers out. It looked like legal papers to me. I turned back to Claudia and she confirmed they were her copy from their lawyer about me and Rex. "What lawyer?" I asked, confused.

"The lawyer we hired to fight to get you kids back." she replied, shaking her head and clucking as if to say, "You silly goose! Of course we had a lawyer."

"You fought for Rex and me?" I asked, blinking back tears I didn't know I had.

Ralph jumped in, interrupting Claudia, "Yes, we did. For seven years we tried to get you back but the Supreme Court said no."

My head was spinning. "The Supreme Court? Like THE Supreme Court of the United States?"

Claudia nodded and said, "It's all there. You should read it."

She turned back to her computer and said, "My screen isn't working right. Will you get down and check the plug? I had to move things around and I don't think it is connected right."

I put down the envelope and rolled up my sleeves, knowing our discussion about the past was over and that I needed to get back to work. I learned from living with Rex that there was no point in forcing conversations that couldn't be spoken.

Late that night, long after Rob and the kids were in bed, I opened the legal envelope again and started reading. After 32 years, I was finally getting the answers to my questions from the lawyers who documented the details of my life.

23. PLAYING SOLOMON

In the early 1970's the state of Oregon developed a new program to address the problem of children languishing in the foster care system. It was a federally funded experiment to fast-track termination of parental rights so children would be available for adoption sooner. It was a 3 year pilot program to see if deadbeat parents either shaped up or shipped out. The reality of foster care is that the older the child, the less attractive to potential adoptive parents they become. And the fiscal reality of foster care is that it costs money to pay people to take care of children. Adoption gets kids off the state payroll. It was a consideration in our case:

"When terminations are viewed as a means of facilitating adoptions, one becomes aware that they will always promote the interests of the state regardless of the particular interest of any single child; terminations aid the state in meeting the demand for 'adoptable' children while also relieving it from financial costs of long-term foster care, homemaker services, and other welfare or public services."

(Oregon Court of Appeals 19 Or.App. 314 pg 4 Wade vs State of Oregon)

Our family got caught up in 'The Great Experiment.' In January of 1973, when I was 5 years-old, the Children Services Division of the Department of Human Resources of the State of Oregon re-assigned us to caseworker John Lawrence. He was a member of a unit of Oregon's Children Services Division funded entirely by the Federal Office of Child Development under a project entitled Freeing Children for Permanent Placement --- also known as the "Termination Project".

My parents had no idea John Lawrence was there to prove they were unfit parents. They thought he was their case worker, helping them care for their children. On May 9, 1973 at ages 7 and 5, Ezra and I were formally made wards of the Circuit Court of the State of Oregon for Multnomah County Juvenile Department. At this time we were still living in the foster home and visiting our parents on the weekends.

Along the legal path, an attorney, B.B. Bouneff, got a call from a judge saying, "These folks don't have a lawyer, and they need one." Mr. Bouneff was a young, idealistic attorney with a strong moral compass that pointed to flagrant misuse of power by the state's Children's Services Department. He agreed to represent my parents. Claudia and Ralph lived on Ralph's income as a dishwasher and Claudia's occasional income selling pens to pay for her medicine. They were not on the welfare rolls. They did live in low-income housing while we were very young, but managed to buy a small house of their own while we were in foster care.

In the court documents, it shows both Ezra and I were considered of normal intelligence, which was the psychiatrists main argument for our being removed from our biological parents care.

In the petition for the Supreme Court of the United States, it says the following:

"Dr. Morrison produced the only evidence concerning the nature and impact of Appellants' (our parents) conditions. He testified that Mr. Wade's intelligence was "borderline," and that the children of parents of "defective intelligence" soon learn they are brighter than their parents and use this to their own detriment."

Dr. Morrison testified, "Claudia was diagnosed as suffering from incurable paranoid schizophrenia and her illness included a systemized set of delusions by which she is able to maintain that as a child she was transported to Earth from the planet La Mordia in the galaxy of Andromeda, and has since the age of 13 been regularly corresponding, by way of a messenger, with her family remaining there. Mrs. Wade also believes that her children will be able to receive messages from La Mordia when they reach adolescence in spite of the fact that they are 'part Earthling.'"

Dr. Morrison also testified that Mrs. Wade's condition would not change in the foreseeable future and that there was no social or mental health services available 'that would help her beyond what she has already received.'

There was no further evidence of how our parents might affect us children. There was no attempt to show that Claudia's schizophrenia or Ralph's low level of intellectual functioning had damaged us in any way. There was also no mention of the arrangement between our foster parents and Ralph and Claudia, which had existed for five years. There was no consideration whether it caused harm to Ezra and me, who were described as bright and normal.

The court records continue, "There is no evidence of physical abuse of the children. It is uncontradicted that Mrs. Wade's condition does not present a danger to the physical well being of the children. There is no indication that the family relationship between Mr. and Mrs. Wade is unstable and it is shown that the parents love their children and are concerned about their welfare. The parent's visitation has been continuous and regular in all kinds of weather and under various adverse conditions. Mrs. Wade realized she, at one time, had been sufficiently ill to need assistance and Mr. Wade helped her obtain hospitalization.

"Except for the time immediately after Mrs. Wade's release from the hospital, the return of the children was never seriously discussed by the State. At that time, Mr. Wade felt the family situation was such that they were unable to care for the children adequately.

"At no other time was there serious discussion

concerning the return of the children, even though the parents were cooperative, the visitations went well, there were no ill effects from the visits, and the physical situation of the family met their needs. In fact, the current caseworker had only made two home visits in one year."

On the other side, the State Deputy District Attorney, Elizabeth Welch, argued that Claudia's mental illness was severe enough to impair her good judgment, and she cited the situation where Ralph once "acknowledged his and his wife's inability to care for their children because of Claudia's 'illness'".

Ms. Welch stated, "Claudia's inability to comprehend the needs of her children is so substantial that during 1971, she suggested that they be 'given' to friends of hers who had had their own children removed from their custody by the juvenile court."

Even Claudia's staunch religious beliefs ended up in court. As a practicing Jehovah's Witness, Claudia had a belief in an "end time" to this life during Christ's reappearance on earth, followed by a millennium of peace. When questioned by State case workers on how she planned to care for her children as they got older, Claudia replied confidently that the second coming of Christ would happen shortly, and when that occurred, everyone's needs would be met.

The Overseer for Claudia's church congregation was called to testify that the Jehovah's Witnesses do have a belief in the second coming of Christ, but also expect parents to fully care for their children.

The District Attorney felt very strongly that Claudia was a clear and present danger to Ezra and me. It was her duty to protect us. Claudia's own history of abuse as a child made Ms. Welch determined to keep us away from not only Claudia, but also her extended family.

B.B. Bouneff as defense council for Ralph and Claudia, was fighting for their rights as parents. Elizabeth Welch as District Attorney was arguing they were unfit as parents. No one took testimony from Ezra and me or asked us what we wanted. We didn't meet either lawyer to be interviewed. Each side's arguments came from reports filed from state social workers. No state worker was aware of the abuse we suffered in foster care. No one ever asked if we were being abused. No lawyers represented our best interests, even though it was our future that was being discussed and litigated.

Our case wound thru the courts in Oregon, ending up being heard in the Supreme Court of the State of Oregon in 1974 where it was found that, "although the state succeeded in establishing by a preponderance of the evidence introduced below that termination would be necessary, the motion for independent counsel for the children should have been allowed."

B.B. Bouneff made a petition to the Supreme Court of the United States, based on the decision from the Oregon State Supreme Court that a legal error was made by lower courts not allowing legal representation for Ezra and me.

Our case was read by the U.S. Supreme Court, but not accepted to be heard. Mr. Bouneff was devastated; worried he had used the wrong legal arguments. He used several different legal points of protest:

1. The State of Oregon used my parent's health issues as the reason to terminate their parental rights.

2. There was insufficient evidence of neglect or abuse to justify the termination of parental rights.

3. Dr. Morrison's evidence of mental unfitness was improperly admitted to the court over an objection founded on the physician-patient privilege. (Ralph and Claudia thought they were getting "check-ups" from a physician.)

There were lawyers to represent the State of Oregon, lawyers to represent Ralph and Claudia, but the previous courts denied the request for a lawyer to represent the best interests of Ezra and me.

After the U.S. Supreme Court declined to hear our case, it was the end of the road. Parental rights were officially terminated on October 22, 1975 when I was 8 and Ezra was 10. The District Attorney was victorious for my brother and me on the day we finally were cleared for adoption. She was glad we could now be adopted by a loving family and begin new lives.

B.B. Bouneff was heartsick for Ralph and Claudia and worried we kids would be stuck in foster care limbo without our parents for years. He ached for Ralph and Claudia, knowing the deck was stacked against them from the beginning.

The following year, a similar case to ours occurred in New York and that lawyer contacted B.B. Bouneff for advice and ended up using Bouneff's arguments for his case before the U.S. Supreme Court and won. That brought a measure of peace to B.B., knowing his argument wasn't flawed, but it did nothing to help us; the wheels were already in motion and no brakes were on our bus.

24. WE'RE NOT DONE YET

In the beginning of our new relationship I dreaded being with Claudia and Ralph in public. I never knew what crazy conversation Claudia was going to start with a stranger or if Ralph was going to be overly friendly with small children, scaring their parents. I relived my experiences with Rex all over again, times two. The first time I told Ralph to stop talking to a 3 year-old, he said, "Why should I? I'm just being friendly. I'm not hurting him."

I leaned over and whispered, "Because the little boy is scared and his parents won't like it."

Ralph argued again that he wasn't hurting anyone, he was just talking to the child. I was stymied and didn't know what to say. Should I explain that people would think Ralph was a pedophile? I didn't want to hurt his feelings or have to explain what a child sex abuser was, but Ralph wasn't going to accept my redirection without a fight. Thankfully, the little boy's parents came and took him away, making my dilemma disappear.

That scene was repeated over and over until I accepted Ralph wasn't going to stop seeking out little kids until I fully explained it and maybe not even then. I might be dealing with his fascination with children until he died. We had the conversation in the car on the way to run errands at the mall. I started casually with, "Hey Ralph, you know how you like to talk to children?"

Ralph replied, "Yeah."

"Well, sometimes that doesn't work so well."

Ralph immediately picked up my line of thought and started his usual argument. "I'm not hurting them. I love children. I'm just being their friend."

I interrupted him, "I know you like kids. You are very good with them and they like you, too. But their parents are worried. Some grown-ups are not as nice to children as you are. Some people do terrible and bad things to kids. When you talk to kids in stores and such, it makes the parents scared because it is their job to protect their children from bad people."

Ralph was thoughtful for a moment, and then he replied, "I would never do bad things to kids. I would never do bad things to anyone."

I reassured him, "I know you wouldn't, but other people don't know how good you are. You are a stranger to them and they have to protect their children from you. It's the law. And I don't want you to get into trouble with the law because you talked to a kid and their parents got worried."

Ralph took that in and sighed knowingly, "Yeah, the law. Ok, I won't talk to kids, but I don't hurt them. I wouldn't ever hurt little children."

I patted his leg and said, "I know. You are a good man."

Our conversation worked and Ralph reigned in his natural public affection for children.

My attempts at changing Claudia's behavior didn't go so well. She didn't accept my simplistic reasoning that it's not appropriate to approach parents of little girls and to tell them if they bought one long skirt, the child could wear that for years instead of buying new clothes as she grows. Claudia refused my explanation that how parents choose to dress their daughters is up to them. Her determination that a world full of little girls tripping on long skirts was a good idea, made me shudder, thinking of the wardrobe I would have been forced to wear if I had lived with Claudia as a child. I thought Virginia's control over my clothes was bad, I couldn't imagine trying to navigate Claudia's ideas on girl's clothes.

Some of the things that I discovered about Ralph and Claudia disturbed me because I found out how much I am exactly like them. For instance, I have always preferred to read while eating at the dinner table. I don't do it because it is rude, but on the rare occasion I am eating alone, I always have a book to read. The first time I took Ralph and Claudia out to eat in a restaurant and Claudia propped up her thick, hard cover book with the salt and pepper shakers, I knew immediately where my quirk came from.

When Ralph described his dream of living off the land in a solar-powered underground home with rain barrels to collect water, the mystery of why I have always been interested in 'earthy' topics was solved.

Shortly after Rex and I were adopted by the Spencers I found a magazine subscription card for Mother Earth News. I carefully printed my name and new address into the tiny letter blocks on the card and slipped the postage paid card into the outgoing mail slot. When my first issue of Mother Earth News arrived, Virginia was flummoxed. Why would a seven year-old kid want a subscription to a hippie magazine about organic gardening and living off the grid? She made me write a letter to Mother Earth explaining I was a child and didn't have money to buy a subscription. I also had to mail back the magazine. I was sad, I wanted to keep the magazine so I could finish reading about underground root cellars. As a foster child watching the hippies next door create their community, I was intrigued by their organic, back-to earth lifestyle. I just didn't know it was in my blood, too.

The revelations went on and on. Everything from my secret dream of rehabbing a school bus and living on the road to my weird childhood preference for eating raw hamburger instead of cooked meat - they did it, thought it and openly discussed it. It turns out I haven't had an original thought in my head my whole life. Who knew? I thought I was unique, an independent person with ideas outside of the conservative Republican home I lived in with the Spencers. I'm not special, I am just my parent's child. The only thing we differ on is I prefer daily showers, brushing my teeth, and wearing clean clothes. The rest of me? Completely a copy of my parental DNA.

After seven years of living in Illinois, our children were in high school and it was time to move them from the sheltered environment of the School for the Deaf to a mainstream school. Rob accepted an appointment at the University of Missouri in Columbia, Missouri. The question of what to do with Ralph and Claudia hung in the air between Rob and me. We were moving. Would they move too? Yep. They did, renting their own small U-Haul truck they followed us to Missouri.

My involvement in Ralph and Claudia's lives naturally got more intense. Claudia felt free to call when their car broke down and needed repairs or when they ran out of money and needed food.

Once they rode the city bus and had to walk several blocks to my house because they decided to surprise me with a drop-in visit. They didn't understand that just because my homeopathic office is in my home doesn't mean I am available to play. After spending a day cooling their heels alone in my living room while I worked in my office, they learned.

I also helped them when their apartment was broken into twice and their meager belongings were taken. Someone stole Claudia's computer along with their tv set and VCR. I couldn't understand why anyone would steal from people who already had so little. It reminded me of Rex almost being killed because he didn't have money. We found out who robbed Ralph and Claudia a few months later when a neighbor in their low-income, subsidized housing complex was evicted and their stuff was piled on the curb for trash pickup. Claudia reclaimed her computer and tv, both she had purchased from the local pawn shop. The VCR must have had more value because it was gone.

Ralph and Claudia's staunch Jehovah's Witness beliefs prevent them from celebrating Christmas, Thanksgiving or any other man-made holidays. As a result, there is no pressure to spend the 4th of July at a backyard barbeque with them. I appreciate the chance to recharge my batteries on quiet holidays with just my husband and children.

Taking them shopping is like trying to herd cats. They each get an idea on where they want to go and they take off on different directions. I sometimes wish it was possible for me to put adult leashes on them. It would lessen the amount of time I spend wandering around Wal-Mart trying to guess where they might be.

I also spend a good amount of time negotiating what I will and won't do for them. If they had their way, I would be their full-time companion. Some days when their public displays of specialness are over the top and I am tired of peeling them away from talking to perfect strangers, I find myself resenting the burden of caring for them. But then they hug me or sincerely thank me for taking them on an outing and I am once again reminded of their goodness and how I need to accept them for who they are. It is a weird experience taking care of my elderly parents who weren't really my parents. Absolutely none of the things that happened to me, to Rex or them was because of anything bad they did. Living with Rex and learning about his disabilities was a training ground for dealing with Claudia and Ralph. I have mellowed in my expectations of what normal is and I continue to work on loving them with the kind of feeling 'Dr. Love' showed me is possible. I admit it is hard work at times.

Claudia still passionately believes she is from the planet La Mordia and that she switched places with an earth girl named Janet Pogue. She refuses to respond to her birth name Janet, which drives her now 94 year-old mother, Lennis, up the wall.

I pay close attention to what Claudia is saying when she starts spitting out names and dates from her near photographic memory. I have a hard time keeping straight which line of family genealogy is from earth and which is from La Mordia. When Claudia starts speaking her in her native La Mordian tongue, Ralph shouts, "Claudia!" and she stops.

Sometimes I just have to laugh at it all.

Whenever we are out, I can expect to be introduced as, "This is our daughter, Haddie. She takes care of us. She has three children. We have three grandchildren and a great-granddaughter."

Their pride in parenting is obvious. The pain is there, too. Recently I was driving them somewhere and I casually commented that they were good parents. I was referring to their present day attempts at showing me love and attention. Ralph fiercely replied, "We would have NEVER given you kids away. We didn't know that was going to happen. We didn't have a choice."

His face was earnest and his elderly voice cracked with emotion.

Claudia nodded in agreement. "That's right. We were tricked. They lied to us. We agreed only to you kids staying at the foster home. We stayed in that awful house for 13 years, hoping you would come back."

She punctuated her statement with a fist on the dash. I was speechless. After all these years, their pain was still there. They hadn't forgotten. I felt tears well up in my eyes and the road ahead of me momentarily got blurry.

"I know," I said, squeezing Ralph's hand. "I know."

I find myself imagining what our lives would have been like if we had all stayed together. How would I have handled growing up surrounded by such colorful characters? Would I be the person I am today? Would I be a better person, with more compassion, or would I have wanted to escape my biological family just as I did my adoptive family?

Mr. Bouneff, my parent's defense attorney, is still practicing law, helping families with adoptions. His phone number is unchanged since our family's case in 1973.

Elizabeth Welch, the district attorney who tried to protect

my brother and me, retired in 2008 as an Oregon State Supreme Court judge in family law, after devoting her entire career to helping children in the courts.

Thousands of children have benefited from their work.

Mr. Bouneff and Ms. Welch became good friends as a result of our case and they debated the merits of our situation for years afterward.

Neither of them has forgotten our situation because there was no easy right answer at the time. All these years later, I still don't know if there is one. What I do know is that my brother was right, the only healing balm that really works is love.

ACKNOWLEDGEMENTS

Thank you to my friends and homeopathic clients who read drafts of this book over the past eight years. Without your continued encouragement I would have shredded this book after the first draft. Thanks for making me stick with it.

I want to hug Patty Wilhite at the Oregon Department of Human Services, Adoption Search and Registry for digging into disintegrating files to find the records of me and my brother's childhood. Thanks for helping me handle what we found.

I did hug B. B. Bouneff to thank him for championing my parent's legal right to raise their children, but can you ever squeeze the stuffing out of someone too much? I think not.

I thank Leslie, Stephanie and their families, Mr. Gross, Brother Davis, The Bingham family, Rob and our children for helping me find my way in this troublesome world. I am blessed.

Lastly, I thank Claudia and Ralph Wade and my beloved brother Rex, for teaching me to release my fears and to let my freak flag fly.

ABOUT THE AUTHOR

Heather Young is an advocate for children and families with
hearing loss and other special needs. She currently resides in
Iowa with her husband and three children.